AF303557

Table of Contents

Introduction

Understanding the stock market is essential to making informed trading decisions. You need to know how to choose the right stocks, which requires an in-depth understanding of a company's annual report and financial statements. Learn how to understand what stock represents in a company and how to determine the true value of any stock. This allows you to make better investing decisions by avoiding the costly mistake of purchasing a company's stock when the market has pushed its share price too high relative to its value.

The workings of the stock market can be confusing. Some people believe investing is a form of gambling and feel that, if you invest, you will likely end up losing your money. These fears can stem from the personal experiences of family members and friends who suffered similar fates or lived through the Great Depression. These feelings are understandable but aren't grounded in facts. Someone who believes in this line of thinking may not have an in-depth understanding of the stock market, why it exists, and how it works.

Other people believe that they should invest for the long run but don't know where to begin. Before learning about how the stock market works, they look at investing like some sort of magic that only a few people know how to use. More often than not, they leave their financial decisions up to professionals and cannot tell you why they own a particular stock or mutual fund.

This investment style could be called blind faith, or perhaps it's limited to a sentiment such as, "This stock is going up—we should buy it." Though it may not seem so on the surface, this group is in far more danger than the first. They tend to invest by following the masses and then wonder why they only achieve mediocrely, or, in some cases, devastating results.

Upon learning a few techniques, the average investor can evaluate the balance sheet of a company and, following a few relatively simple calculations, arrive at their interpretation of the real value of a company and its stock. This allows an investor to look at a stock and know that it is worth, for instance, $40 per share. This gives each investor the freedom to determine when the market has undervalued stocks, increasing their long-term returns substantially, or overvalued it, making it a poor investment candidate.

A stock market, equity market or share market is the aggregation of buyers and sellers of stocks (also called shares), which represent ownership claims on businesses; these may include securities listed on a public stock exchange, as well as stock that is only traded privately, such as shares of private companies which are sold to investors through equity crowdfunding platforms. Investment in the stock market is most often done via stock brokerages and electronic trading platforms. Investment is usually made with an investment strategy in mind.

Trade-in stock markets mean the transfer (in exchange for money) of a stock or security from a seller to a buyer. This requires these two parties to agree on a price. Equities (stocks or shares) confer an ownership interest in a particular company.

Investing is a way to set aside money while you are busy with life and have that money work for you so that you can fully reap the rewards of your labor in the future. Investing is a means to a happier ending. Legendary investor Warren Buffett defines investing as "...the process of laying out money now to receive more money in the future.", The goal of investing is to put your money to work in one or more types of investment vehicles in the hopes of growing your money over time.

Investing is defined as the act of committing money or capital to an endeavor with the expectation of obtaining an additional income or profit. Unlike consuming, investing earmarks money for the future, hoping that it will grow over time. Investing, however, also comes with the risk of losses. Investing in the stock market is the most common way for beginners to gain investment experience.

Definition of 'Stock Market'

Definition: It is a place where shares of pubic listed companies are traded. The primary market is where companies float shares to the general public in an initial public offering (IPO) to raise capital.

Description: Once new securities have been sold in the primary market, they are traded in the secondary market—where one investor buys shares from another investor at the prevailing market price or whatever price both the buyer and seller agree upon. The secondary market or the stock exchanges are regulated by the regulatory authority.

A stock exchange facilitates stock brokers to trade company stocks and other securities. A stock may be bought or sold only if it is listed on an exchange. Thus, it is the meeting place of the stock buyers and sellers. India's premier stock exchanges are the Bombay Stock Exchange and the National Stock Exchange.

A stock market (also known as an equity market or share market), is a collection of buyers and sellers of stocks. These stocks represent ownership interests in companies. These may include publicly or privately traded securities. The New York Stock Exchange (NYSE) is an example of a share market.

Usually, large companies will list their stock on a stock exchange because it makes their shares more liquid (i.e., easy to buy and sell), which investors love. This liquidity also attracts international investors.

Stock Market

A stock market is a place where people buy/sell shares of publicly listed companies. It offers a platform to facilitate the seamless exchange of shares. In simple terms, if A wants to sell shares of Reliance Industries, the stock market will help him to meet the seller who is willing to buy Reliance Industries. However, it is important to note that a person can trade in the stock market only through a registered intermediary known as a stockbroker. The buying and selling of shares take place through an electronic medium. We will discuss more the stockbrokers at a later point.

Types Of Stocks

Stock

A stock (or a share) is an ownership interest in the underlying business. If you are the owner of the stock, you own a proportionate stake of the company whose stock you own. For E.g. if you own 1000 shares in HDFC Bank, you own 0.00003955% (No. of shares you own / No. of shares of HDFC bank in issue) of the bank.

Growth

Companies that consistently manage to grow their profits faster than their industry peers are called growth stocks. Their faster growth is generally the result of some sustainable competitive advantages. Since they need to constantly fund their growth, they typically pay out little or no dividends. The investors are rewarded from appreciation in stock price. Since competitors can emulate them and eliminate their competitive advantage, growth stocks are riskier than some of the categories we discuss next.

Value

Stocks available at a significant discount to their intrinsic value fall under this category. These are sound businesses in sectors that are not favored by the market presently. Some of them pay a significant share of their profits as dividends or resort to sharing buybacks when their shares are out of favor.

Dividend Yield

These are companies that generate a significant amount of cash in the business and do not have enough profitable opportunities to deploy the cash. So, they return most of it to the shareholders in the form of dividends.

Cyclical

These are companies whose profits are linked to economic cycles. They report significant profits when economic growth is strong and struggle to report profits when economic growth slows down. Typical examples are commodity companies in metals, cement, oil & gas, etc.

Information Sources On Stocks

An investor can gather information on the stock from various sources. Some of them are mentioned below:

Red Herring Prospectus (RHP)

This is the most important information source on any company and the best place to start. It contains industry overview, company background, risk factors, management background, management discussion, and analysis (MD&A) that gives an outlook of the business going forward and detailed financial statements. RHP's are available on the SEBI website.

Annual Reports

Publicly listed companies publish detailed reports annually that include industry overview, company background, company strategy, business outlook, and detailed financial statements of the current and preceding financial year. Annual reports are available on the respective company websites.

Quarterly Results

Publicly listed companies publish quarterly reports of financial performance with the stock exchanges. They also contain business segment-wise information, data on promoter pledging of shares, and non-recurring items that impacted financial performance in the quarter.

Investor Presentations

Many publicly listed companies provide detailed investor presentations that cover company background, company strategy, business outlook, and detailed financial statements of the current and preceding financial period.

Earnings Conference Calls

Many companies conduct conference calls after quarterly results wherein management provides guidance of performance over the medium term and take questions from investors and analysts.

Management Interviews In Print/TV

Management interviews provide clues on management focus on performance, transparency, and shareholder friendliness.

Facts

Stock is an ownership in a business or a company. There are different types of stocks such as growth, dividend yield, value, and

cyclical stocks. Information on stocks can be collected from annual reports, earnings call, management interviews, and investor presentations.

Corporate Actions In The Stock Market

Dividend

Cash-rich companies which do not have adequate opportunity to deploy cash in lucrative business opportunities return a portion of cash to its stockholders. Most often, dividends are paid out of profits though it is not strictly necessary. Dividends are announced periodically (semi-annually, annually, etc). Generally, high growth companies do not pay many dividends, while stable cash-generating businesses do. To be eligible to receive dividends, one should own the stock on the record date.

Stock Split

It is a scenario when a company announces that it is splitting the face value of its shares. Thus, if the face value is Rs 10 and the company announces a 1:5 stock split, the new shares will have a face value of Rs 2. The stockholder receives 5 stocks for each stock that he owned. The market price of the stock falls but the market capitalization of the company does not change meaningfully.

Bonus Issue

These are free shares that the stockholders of the company receive against the shares that they already own. Bonus shares are issued out of the reserves in shareholder funds. Companies announce a ratio by which new shares are allotted to existing stockholders. If the ratio is 3:1, the stockholder receives 3 shares for each share held.

Buyback

A company can offer to buy back its shares from the existing stockholders either because it thinks the share price is too low or because it has surplus capital that it cannot put to good use that it plans to return to the shareholders. Buybacks reduce the number of shares in issue and lead to an increase in EPS.

Rights Issue

In this, a company offers new shares to all the existing stockholders in the ratio of their holding in the company. Shareholders are offered new shares at a discount to encourage them to apply to the issue. This is a primary issue in which the money paid by the shareholder accrues to the company. A 3:1 rights issue indicates that the stockholder can buy 1 share for every 3 shares that he owns in the company.

Major Stock Exchanges

There are two main stock exchanges in India where the majority of the trades take place - the Bombay Stock Exchange (BSE) and the National Stock Exchange (NSE). Apart from these two exchanges, there are some other regional stock exchanges like Bangalore Stock Exchange, Madras Stock Exchange, etc but these exchanges do not play a meaningful role anymore.

National Stock Exchange (NSE)

NSE is the leading stock exchange in India where one can buy/sell shares of publicly listed companies. It was established in the year 1992 and is located in Mumbai. NSE has a flagship index named as NIFTY50. The index comprises of the top 50 companies based on its trading volume and market capitalization. This index is widely used by investors in India as well as globally as the barometer of the Indian capital markets.

Bombay Stock Exchange (BSE)

BSE is Asia's first as well as the oldest stock exchange in India. It was established in 1875 and is located in Mumbai. It has a total of ~5,295 companies listed out of which ~3,972 are available for trading as on August 21, 2017. BSE Sensex is the flagship index of BSE. It measures the performance of the 30 largest, most liquid, and financially stable companies across key sectors.

Types Of Financial Intermediaries In The Stock Market

From the time an investor places his order to buy shares till the time it is transferred to his Demat account, several corporate entities are involved to ensure a smooth transaction. These entities are known as financial intermediaries and they work according to the rules and regulations prescribed by SEBI. Some of the financial intermediaries are discussed below:

Stock Broker

A stockbroker knew as a dealer is a professional individual who buys/sells shares on behalf of its clients. A stockbroker is registered as a trading member with the stock exchange and holds a stockbroking license. They operate under the guidelines prescribed by SEBI. An individual needs to open a trading/DEMAT account to transact in the financial market.

Depository And Depository Participants

A Depository is a financial intermediary that offers the service of the DEMAT account. A DEMAT account will have all the shares that an investor owns in an electronic format. In India, there are only two depositaries which offer DEMAT account services - National Securities Depository Limited (NSDL) and Central Depository Services (India) Limited (CDSL). An investor cannot directly go to the depositary to open the DEMAT account. He needs to appoint a Depository Participant (DP). According to

SEBI guidelines, banks, financial institutions and members of stock exchanges registered with SEBI can become DPs.

Banks

Banks help to transfer funds from a bank account to a trading account. The client needs to categorically mention which bank account has to be linked to the trading account to the stockbroker at the time of opening the trading account.

National Security Clearing Corporation Ltd (NSCCL) And Indian Clearing Corporation Ltd (ICCL)

NSCCL and ICCL are 100% subsidiaries of the National Stock Exchange and Bombay Stock Exchange respectively. They ensure guaranteed settlement of transactions carried in stock exchanges. The clearing corporation ensures there are no defaults either from buyers' or sellers' side.

DEMAT Account And Trading Account

To trade inequities, it is mandatory to have a DEMAT account as well as the Trading account.

DEMAT Account

DEMAT account or dematerialized account allows holding shares in electronic form instead of taking physical possession of certificates. It is mandatory to have a DEMAT account to trade in shares. DEMAT account holds all the investments an individual makes in shares, exchange-traded funds, bonds, government securities, and mutual funds in one place.

Trading Account

A trading account is used to place buy/sell orders in the stock market. One can open their trading account with a stockbroker who is registered with SEBI. An order can be placed either through an online or offline mode. In the online mode, one can buy/sell stocks through the trading terminal provided by the broker whereas; in the offline mode, an individual can ask its broker to place an order on his/her behalf.

What Is A Long Position?

In a long position, the owner benefits when the stock or share gains in value. The potential profit is unlimited. So the "long" position is said to be "bullish." When the stock is down, the most that the owner can lose is the amount of money he has originally paid for it. Since it is impossible to lose more, it is said that the owners have "limited liability."

Long Position Example

Suppose a share is purchased at $60 if the share value doesn't change the owner's profit will be $0. If the share grows in value up to $100, the owner's profit is $40. If the share price drops to $30, the owner's loss will be $30.

In Short Selling the borrower borrows one stock from an owner in exchange for an IOU and then sells it to a buyer. When the market value of the share is down, the borrower buys it and returns to the original owner. Say for example that a short seller borrows 1 GM Stock from the owner in exchange for the borrower's IOU. The borrower sells 1 GM share to a buyer for $60. If the market value of 1 GM drops to $50, the borrower gets $10.

Long Position Example Stock Market

This way the person, who is in the "short selling" position, gains a profit when the share price drops in value. The maximum profit is equal to the amount the share the investor originally paid. However, the maximum potential loss can be unlimited. That's why short selling is considered to be "bearish."

What Is A Short Position?

In a short position, the investor expects that the price of the stock will decrease in the short term. To set up a short sell transaction, the investor borrows the shares from an owner and then sells it to another investor. The investor must ultimately return the stock he borrows. The investor is borrowing and selling the stock at a high price and then later buys the stock from the market when the price falls. He then returns the stock to the owner.

Short Selling Example

Suppose the borrowed share has a present value of $60; if the share price doesn't change, the short seller's profit will be $0. However, if the borrowed share's price goes up in value up to $70, the short seller's loss will be (-$10). If the borrowed share' price drops in value up to $50, the short seller will make a $10 profit.

Stock Market Basics: What Beginner Investors Should Know

Stock Market Basics

The stock market is made up of exchanges, like the New York Stock Exchange and the Nasdaq. Stocks are listed on a specific exchange, which brings buyers and sellers together and acts as a market for the shares of those stocks. The exchange tracks the supply and demand and directly related, the price of each stock. (Need to back up a bit? Read our explainer about stocks.)

But this isn't your typical market, and you can't show up and pick your shares off a shelf the way you select produce at the grocery store. Individual traders are typically represented by brokers these days, that's often an online broker. You place your stock trades through the broker, which then deals with the exchange on your behalf. (Need a broker? See our analysis of the best stock brokers for beginners.)

The NYSE and the Nasdaq are open from 9:30 a.m. to 4 p.m. Eastern, with premarket and after-hours trading sessions also available, depending on your broker.

Understanding The Stock Market

When people refer to the stock market being up or down, they're generally referring to one of the major market indexes.

A market index tracks the performance of a group of stocks, which either represents the market as a whole or a specific sector of the market, like technology or retail companies. You're likely to hear most about the S&P 500, the Nasdaq composite and the Dow Jones Industrial Average; they are often used as proxies for the performance of the overall market.

Investors use indexes to benchmark the performance of their portfolios and, in some cases, to inform their stock trading decisions. You can also invest in an entire index through index funds and exchange-traded funds, or ETFs, which track a specific index or sector of the market. Read more about ETFs here.

Stock Trading Information

Most investors would be well-advised to build a diversified portfolio of stocks or stock index funds and hold on to it through good times and bad. But investors who like a little more actively engage in stock trading. Stock trading involves buying and selling stocks frequently in an attempt to time the market.

The goal of stock traders is to capitalize on short-term market events to sell stocks for a profit or buy stocks at a low. Some stock traders are day traders, which means they buy and sell several times throughout the day. Others are simply active traders, placing a dozen or more trades per month. (Interested in individual stocks? View our list of the best-performing stocks this year.)

Investors who trade stocks do extensive research, often devoting hours a day to following the market. They rely on technical analysis, using tools to chart a stock's movements in an attempt to find trading opportunities and trends. Many online brokers offer stock trading information, including analyst reports, stock research, and charting tools.

What Is The Stock Exchange?

A stock exchange is a marketplace where securities, such as stocks and bonds, are bought and sold. Bonds are typically traded Over-the-Counter (OTC), but some corporate bonds can be traded on stock exchanges. Stock exchanges allow companies to raise capital and investors to make informed decisions using real-time price information. Exchanges can be a physical location or an electronic trading platform. Though people are typically familiar with the image of the trading floor, many exchanges now use electronic trading.

Purpose Of Stock Exchanges

Stock exchanges act as an agent for the economy by facilitating trade and disseminating information. Below are some of the ways exchanges contribute:

1. Raising Capital

Through initial public offerings (IPO) or issuing of new shares, companies can raise capital to fund operations and expansion projects. This provides companies with avenues to increase growth.

2. Corporate Governance

Companies that are publicly listed on a stock exchange must conform to reporting standards that are set by regulating bodies. This includes having to regularly and publicly report their financial statements and earnings to their shareholders. The actions of a company's management are constantly under public scrutiny and directly affect the value of the company. Public reporting helps ensure that management will make decisions that benefit the goals of the company and its shareholders, thereby acting efficiently.

3. Economic Efficiency

In addition to encouraging management efficiency, exchanges also facilitate economic efficiency through the allocation of capital. Stock exchanges provide an avenue for individuals to invest their cash, as opposed to merely saving these funds. This means that the capital that would otherwise be untouched is utilized towards economic benefits, resulting in a more efficient economy.

Exchanges also provide liquidity, as it is relatively easy to sell one's holdings. By providing liquidity and real-time price information on company shares, the stock exchange also encourages an efficient market by allowing investors to actively decide the value of companies through supply and demand.

Notable Stock Exchanges

1. New York Stock Exchange (NYSE)

Founded in 1792, the New York Stock Exchange is by far the largest in the world. As of March 2018, the NYSE's market capitalization was US$23.12 trillion.

2. NASDAQ

Founded in 1971, NASDAQ is a US-based stock exchange. With a market capitalization of US$10.93 trillion as of March 2018, it is the second-largest in the world by market capitalization. Many techs and growth firms choose to be listed on the NASDAQ.

3. Shanghai Stock Exchange (SSE)

Founded in November 1990, the Shanghai Stock Exchange is the fourth-largest exchange in the world. It reported a market capitalization of US$5.01 trillion in March 2018. There are two types of stocks listed on the SSE, 'A-shares' and 'B shares'. Shares are quoted in RMB, with trading in A-shares historically restricted to domestic investors. In July 2018, China announced additional plans to allow foreign investors to access A-shares through domestic brokerages. B shares are quoted in USD and are open to domestic and foreign investors alike.

Introduction To Primary Market

The primary market is a market wherein corporates issue new securities to raise funds. The company which issues its shares is called issuer and the process of issuing shares to the public is known as a public issue or Initial Public Offer (IPO). This entire process involves various intermediaries such as Merchant Banker, Bankers to the Issue, Underwriters, and Registrars to the Issue. All these intermediaries are registered with SEBI.

When a company issues new securities that did not previously exist on any exchange, it is issuing securities to the primary market. Undergoing an IPO is an example of this. The company offers securities to the investors to raise capital and becomes listed on the stock exchange.

Steps To Be Followed By Companies Going For An IPO

1. The company appoints a merchant banker for the IPO process. The merchant banker assists the company in the IPO process.

2. The company has to apply to SEBI with a registration statement. This statement has details about the business of the company, the reason for coming out with an IPO, and the financial details of the company.

3. Once SEBI receives the registration statement, it decides whether the company should be allowed to go for an IPO or not.

4. After the company gets initial approval from SEBI, it needs to prepare the Draft Red Herring Prospectus (DRHP). DRHP is a document which consists of information about the business of the company and the industry that it operates in. This document gets circulated to the public. It includes details such as the estimated size of the IPO, estimated number of shares being offered to the public, how does the company plan to utilize the funds, financial statement of the company, promoter details, etc.

5. The company now has to advertise about the IPO through TV and print advertisements to build awareness about the company and its IPO offering. This process is called the IPO roadshow.

6. The company or the issuer of the IPO has to decide the price band between which the company would like to go public. For example, the company has decided on a price band of Rs 200-

205. So, if an investor wishes to invest in the IPO, he can choose to buy shares at a price anywhere between 200 and 205.

7. After the price band is fixed, the company has to officially open the window so that the public can subscribe for shares. The subscribers can bid for an IPO within the price band decided by the company. This is also called as Book Building.

8. After the subscribing window is closed (which is generally open for 2-3 days), the price point at which the issue gets listed is decided. The shares are then listed on the respective stock exchanges.

Procedure To Apply For An IPO

1. The subscriber compulsorily needs a DEMAT account to apply for an IPO. He also needs to apply for ASBA (Applications Supported by Blocked Amount) through the bank to which he has linked his trading and DEMAT account.

2. One can apply for an IPO offline as well as online.

3. In offline mode, the subscriber needs to collect the IPO form from the stockbroker and submit the duly filled form. The broker will then submit the form to your bank to which you have linked the trading account.

4. In online mode, one can directly login to net banking services of the bank to which he has linked his trading account and apply for the IPO.

Introduction To Secondary Market

The secondary market is where the securities issued in the primary market are bought and sold on the stock exchanges - Bombay Stock Exchange (BSE), National Stock Exchange (NSE), and others. BSE and NSE are the most widely traded exchanges in India with a market capitalization of Rs 1,25,18,954 crore and Rs 12,282,127 crore respectively.

After a company undergoes an IPO, its shares continue to be traded between investors on the market. This is referred to as the secondary market. The company is no longer involved in any of these transactions. The stock exchange facilitates trade between buyers and sellers in the secondary market.

How To Evaluate Stocks And Stock Ratios

If you're interested in buying single stocks, you can't simply follow your gut and expect everything to work out for the best. Instead, you have to lean on tried and true investing and trading strategies to remove emotion and guide your buy and sell decisions. Financial ratios give you insight into a company's fundamentals. These financial performance measures let you assess a company's health on its own or compared to an industry peer group.

Here's What You Need To Know To Put Some Of The Most Popular Stock Ratios To Work.

Qualitative And Quantitative Analysis

When investing, you should never buy or sell based on a single input. Instead, you should look at the company holistically to assess whether you think the share price is headed up or down.

Technical analysis focuses on how the stock has performed recently, compared to other stocks. Fundamental analysis zeros in on the financial metrics behind the company, not just what the stock price is doing.

I'm a huge fan of fundamental analysis and make my own investment decisions based on fundamentals. You can take your fundamental analysis a step further by separating qualitative and quantitative aspects of the underlying business.

Use Quantitative Analysis

Quantitative analysis means a pure focus on the numbers. Financial ratios are generally based on these. The numbers you get from the income, balance sheet, and cash flow statements are all sources of data for quantitative analysis. That's what we'll focus on with the ratios below.

But don't forget about qualitative analysis. You can't put everything into a number. The qualitative analysis takes you through other important aspects of the company. For example, the numbers alone won't tell you a lot about competitors, technology changes, or other market threats or opportunities.

Look at the whole package when your money is on the line. Never just a single number or factor or gut instinct alone.

Key Financial Ratios When Buying Stocks

Before you click the "Buy" button, you'll want to check out some key financial ratios and compare them to industry peers. The most important ratios look at the company's income and its ability to remain solvent.

The most commonly cited ratio may be the price-to-earnings ratio, also called the P/E or PE ratio. This ratio looks at the share price compared to the earnings per share. It's a great way to compare stocks with peers to get an idea of whether it may be overpriced, underpriced, or in line with other companies in the industry.

Stock Ratio Categories

The two most common categories of stock ratios look at earnings and the balance sheet. These are essential indicators of a business's financial health. Here's a glance at some of the stock market ratios you are most likely to come across and how to put them to work. These are the ones that help us understand the valuation, profitability, and liquidity of a company.

Valuation: Price To Earnings (P/E)

This is a hugely popular metric. To calculate P/E, divide the market value (stock price) by the company's earnings per share.

Valuation: Price To Earnings Growth (PEG)

The PEG ratio is a favorite of growth and GARP investors. PEG divides the P/E by the growth rate of the company's earnings. A low PEG below 1 indicates a stock may be undervalued. A high PEG indicates a stock could be overpriced.

Valuation: Price To Sales (P/S)

The price-to-sales ratio divides the market capitalization by the company's 12-month revenue. A low P/S compared to other companies in the industry indicates a company may be an attractive investment.

Valuation: Price to Book (P/B)

One of my favorite ratios is P/B. I have a favorite ratio what can I say?, This ratio compares the stock price to the company's book value (assets minus liabilities). A low P/B could indicate a good buy. If the book value per share is higher than the stock price, it's a solid indication of an undervalued stock.

Valuation: Dividend Yield

The dividend yield is the percentage return of a stock's price. It is determined by dividing the annual dividend by the current stock price. While stocks are riskier than bonds and savings accounts, you could compare dividend yield to the payout on a bond or savings account. The high dividend yield is a good thing if you care about earning cash flow from your portfolio. However, very high yields may not be sustainable.

Valuation: Dividend Payout

This ratio compares the company's dividend payout to its net income. It tells you what percent of profits are paid to investors.

This isn't necessarily a good or bad thing, but it's good information to know. If a company gives too much in dividends, it is less likely to grow. If it isn't paying any dividends, it is reinvesting every dollar back into growing the business.

Profitability: Return On Assets (ROA)

This ratio helps investors judge how much money a company makes compared to its assets. It tells you how to lean and nimble a company is. Or how much it has wrapped up in the business itself. Comparing companies across the industry, you can use this metric to judge how efficient a company is with its resources.

Profitability: Return On Equity (ROE)

ROE is a stricter measure of how well a company uses its resources. ROE is found by dividing the company's net income by shareholders' equity. You could also call ROE a return on net assets.

Profitability: Profit Margin

This is another hugely popular metric. The profit margin shows what percent a company earns in profits compared to its total revenues. A high-profit margin means a company is keeping a larger percentage of the revenue it brings in. Higher profit margins than industry peers can indicate that a company is better at managing costs.

Liquidity: Current Ratio

The current ratio divides current assets by current liabilities. Current assets are highly liquid, like cash and equivalents. Current liabilities are debts due within one year. This tells you if a company has enough money to pay the bills. The acid test, sometimes called the quick ratio, takes into account fewer of the company's assets and divides that by the current liabilities. This is an even stricter measure of financial health.

Ways To Analyze Stock

As investors, learning how to evaluate a stock is extremely important. Proper evaluation of stock means attempting to value its current and future earnings, examine its place in its industry, the competitive environment around the company, and also external stock market conditions. Investors depend on stock analysis to find potentially profitable stocks. Common ways to analyze stock include technical and fundamental analysis. Several components fall under fundamental analysis, including examination of a company's price-to-earnings ratio, earnings per share, book value, and return on equity. Many investors also use the recommendations of financial analysts to analyze a stock. The type of stock analysis you implement is based on personal preference. Understand the different ways to analyze a stock to find the method that best fits your financial objectives.

What Is Fundamental Analysis ?

It is the approach whereby an individual tries to compute the intrinsic value of a stock by looking at the fundamental economic factors that are likely to impact the value.

Factors Important For The Analysis

Following are the factors that are important for conducting the fundamental analysis:

1. Parameters From Balance Sheet And Profit & Loss: This includes revenues, expenses, and profit

2. Growth Prospects Of The Company: This consists of an understanding of the market, product profile, customer profile, concentration, and the likes.

3. Competitive Factors For The Company: This includes an understanding of the competitive landscape of the company, including competitors, market share, barriers to entry, pricing power, etc.

4. Expected Return On Equity Or Assets: This includes the industry average and is ideally higher than the Sensex (or any other benchmark) returns since inception.

The Goal Of The Analysis

The purpose of this analysis is to establish a value of the stock that would factor in all the underlying factors mentioned above. The approach doesn't look at the short-term pricing and doesn't take into account the short-term trade swings. The plan is for long-term investment as it tends to make time for the intrinsic value to be realized. In this approach, the factors are forward-looking expectations, and the model is build to arrive at the valuation based on backward and forward-looking information.

What Is Technical Analysis ?

It is the approach in which an individual evaluates investments purely on the market activity surrounding them. The method doesn't involve looking at the actual operations or value of the company.

Factors Important For The Analysis

Following are the factors that are important for conducting the technical analysis:

- ❖ Historical price of the stock
- ❖ Historical trading volume
- ❖ Industry trading trends

Some Tools Used In Technical Analysis

1. There are several tools available in techniques such as simple moving averages are indicators that help assess the stock's trend by averaging the daily price over a fixed period.

2. Besides, there are few momentum-based indicators, such as Bollinger Bands, Chaikin Money Flow, Stochastics, and Moving Average Convergence/Divergence (MACD).

3. Each of these unique tools provides buy and sell signals based on their criteria.

The Goal Of The Analysis

The purpose of the analysis is to capitalize on pricing opportunities and trends that are identifiable in the market for each share. The methodology is based on the historical price of the stock, historical market activity, past trading volumes to identify the pattern.

How Is Fundamental Analysis Conducted?

As seen previously, the fundamental analysis seeks to find the enterprise value of the company. Thus, the approach uses economic factors. While conducting fundamental analysis, the following route is adopted:

- ❖ Economic Analysis
- ❖ Industry Analysis
- ❖ Company Analysis

Assumptions In The Analysis

Over the long-term, the stock price tends to reach its intrinsic value. Gain can be made by purchasing an under-valued stock and then wait for the market to take it to its real value. The technique is adopted by value investors looking for buy and hold strategy.

Steps To Carry Out The Fundamental Analysis

Step 1: Perform Industry Analysis:

An analyst/investor should dig out and find everything about the sector in which the company operates. The study will give output such as:

- ❖ Sector growth rate
- ❖ Key drivers for growth
- ❖ Contribution to the GDP by the industry
- ❖ Sector trends
- ❖ Demand and Supply analysis

Step 2: Conduct A Company Analysis

In this step, an analyst is supposed to understand the inside out of the company using different financial tools such as ratio analysis horizontal analysis, vertical analysis, etc. The study will give output such as:

- ❖ Trend evaluation – percentage increase/decrease relative to the base year
- ❖ Areas where the company has applied its resources
- ❖ Proportions in which the funds are distributed to different heads
- ❖ Understanding the changes in the financial situation

Step 3: Conduct Financial Modeling

In this step, an analyst is required to forecast the future of the company for the foreseeable future, i.e., Three to seven years. An analyst may need a lot of information and assumptions in this step. This may be availed with the help of the management interview. The objective of the step is to analyze how the financial statements and the stock price will look in the future.

Step 4: Carry Out Valuation

There are many techniques for valuation that can be used. Many of the methods are dependent on the type of company and industry. Some of the ways are – Discounted Cash Flow (DCF), Relative valuation (includes Price to Earnings Multiple, Price to Book Value Multiple, etc.), and Sum of the parts (SOTP).

Discounted Cash Flow Analysis

In this method, the analyst arrives at the intrinsic value. The ways and procedures are exciting, and an analyst can always be innovative with the approach. Once, you arrive at the intrinsic share price for the company; the following is the interpretation.

If Market Price (MP) > Intrinsic Price (IP) = stock is overvalued and the analyst should recommend sell or the investor should sell the stock

If MP < IP = stock is undervalued, and the analyst should recommend buying, or the investor should buy the stock

Relative Valuation Analysis

In this approach, analyst/investor values the company by comparing it to the peer group. Following parameters are used in the approach:

- ❖ PE Ratio (Price to Earnings Ratio)
- ❖ Earnings Per Share (EPS)
- ❖ EV/EBITDA
- ❖ EV/Sales, etc.

How Is A Technical Analysis Conducted?

Technical analysis, as mentioned above, is a method of evaluating securities. However, in this method, the game is dependent upon the stats generated by the market. Thus, charts and patterns are the bread and butter for such an approach. Following are the characteristics of technical analysis are:

❖ Uses past price movement to predict the future price movement

❖ Trends and Patterns play a significant role

❖ The market price is the bible

❖ Fundamental factors may not impact

Rules Of Technical Analysis

Following are the three golden rules for technical analysis:

1. **First Rule:** Prices discount information available to the public

2. **Second Rule:** Price movement is generally based on the trend that can be predicted (to some extent) using technical tools

3. **The Third Rule:** Price Trends are likely to repeat themselves

Steps To Carry Out The Technical Analysis

Step 1: Identify The Security That Interest You

Basic research on trending sector shall help an analyst/investor (trader) to decide on the stock to buy or sell.

Step 2: Identify The Strategy

Remember, one approach doesn't fit all the stocks, and thus you must have variation based on the share, its characteristics.

Step 3: Select The Right Trading Account

This step is essential to ensure that the brokerage or the charges involved are within your budget and are reasonable.

Step 4: Understand The Tools And Interfaces

An analyst/investor (trade) is supposed to select the tools that fit your trading requirements and strategies. You can always check the web for freely available tools.

Step 5: Conduct Trade On Simulation First

While making investments by technical approach, an investor should first try their strategy on the selected stock with the help of a simulation tool or tools such as excel. Once the testing of the approach is conducted, only then you should shift to trade with real money.

Step 6: Always Have A Stop Loss

A stop-loss allows you to cut on your losses automatically if the stock moves opposite than anticipated. This helps in holding a losing trade. Having a stop loss enables an investor to remain disciplined.

Fundamental Analysis

Advantages

1. The methods used in the fundamental analysis are based on financial data and thus eliminates room for personal bias.

2. The approach considers long-term economic, demographic, technological, and, consumer trends.

3. The analysis has a systematic approach with different statistical and analytical tools that help in arriving at the final Buy/Sell recommendation

4. Rigorous accounting and financial analysis allows an investor to gauge a better understanding of the company and its practices

Disadvantages

1. Conducting industry analysis, valuation is not everyone's cup of tea and needs a good amount of hard work, patience, and time.

2. Assumptions play a vital role in forecasting financials. Thus, things may go wrong if the assumptions are not rationale.

Technical Analysis

Advantages

Following are the benefits of the approach:

1. Provides Insights On Volume: It goes on without saying that demand and supply govern the market dynamics. Thus, knowing the volume helps you gauge how the overall market works. Tells about the entry and exit points with the help of charts and patterns

2. Provides Current Information: Price reflects information about an asset. Patterns give a directional view and act as a guide to direct your buy and sell decisions.

Disadvantages

1. Many indicators often spoil the chart thereby by producing confusing signals that may affect the analysis

2. Fundamentals remain ignored: The approach does not take into account the underlying fundamentals of a company. This can prove risky over the long-term.

Which Approach Is Suitable For You?

Trading style and attitude go in sync. Your attitude helps you understand what kind of investment approach will suit you. Often investors are seen combining both these approaches and ending nowhere. When it comes to choosing between the two, several factors should be considered.

1. Time Horizon Is Essential To Consider: Fundamental analysis is a long-term strategy, whereas technical analysis is more short-term in nature.

2. Understand Your Investment Approach: Are you an investor or a trader? Fundamental analysis is investing in the business because you believe in the product/service and believe the price to reach its intrinsic value over tie.

3. How Much Time You Can Give: Trading needs active time and management on the part of the investor. On the other hand, the fundamental approach asks for patience.

4 Key Steps To Evaluate Any Stock

One note before we dive in: Stocks are considered long-term investments because they carry quite a bit of risk; you need time to weather any ups and downs and benefit from long-term gains. That means investing in stocks is best for the money you won't need in at least the next five years. (Elsewhere we outline better options for short-term savings.)

1. Gather Your Stock Research Materials

Start by reviewing the company's financials. This is called quantitative research, and it begins with pulling together a few documents that companies are required to file with the U.S. Securities and Exchange Commission:

Form 10-K: An annual report that includes key financial statements that have been independently audited. Here you can review a company's balance sheet, its sources of income and how it handles its cash, and its revenues and expenses.

Form 10-Q: A quarterly update on operations and financial results.

Short on time? You'll find highlights from the above filings and important financial ratios on your brokerage firm's website or major financial news websites. (If you don't have a brokerage account, here's how to open one.) This information will help you compare a company's performance against other candidates for your investment dollars.

2. Narrow Your Focus

These financial reports contain a ton of numbers and it's easy to get bogged down. Zero in on the following line items to become familiar with the measurable inner workings of a company:

Revenue: This is the amount of money a company brought in during the specified period. It's the first thing you'll see on the income statement, which is why it's often referred to as the "top line." Sometimes revenue is broken down into "operating revenue" and "nonoperating revenue." Operating revenue is most telling because it's generated from the company's core business.

Nonoperating revenue often comes from one-time business activities, such as selling an asset.

Net income: This "bottom line" figure so-called because it's listed at the end of the income statement is the total amount of money a company has made after operating expenses, taxes, and depreciation are subtracted from revenue. Revenue is the equivalent of your gross salary, and net income is comparable to what's leftover after you've paid taxes and living expenses.

Earnings And Earnings Per Share (EPS): When you divide earnings by the number of shares available to trade, you get earnings per share. This number shows a company's profitability on a per-share basis, which makes it easier to compare with other companies. When you see earnings per share followed by "(TM)" that refers to the "trailing twelve months."

Earnings are far from a perfect financial measurement because it doesn't tell you how or how efficiently the company uses its capital. Some companies take those earnings and reinvest them in the business. Others pay them out to shareholders in the form of dividends.

Price-Earnings Ratio (P/E): Dividing a company's current stock price by its earnings per share — usually over the last 12 months — gives you a company's trailing P/E ratio. Dividing the stock price by forecasted earnings from Wall Street analysts gives you the forward P/E. This measure of a stock's value tells you how much investors are willing to pay to receive $1 of the company's current earnings. Keep in mind that the P/E ratio is derived from the potentially flawed earnings per share calculation, and analyst estimates are notoriously focused on the short term. Therefore it's not a reliable stand-alone metric.

Return On Equity (ROE) And Return On Assets (ROA): Return on equity reveals, in percentage terms, how much profit a company generates with each dollar shareholders have invested. The equity is shareholder equity. Return on assets shows what percentage of its profits the company generates with each dollar of its assets. Each is derived from dividing a company's annual net income by one of those measures. These percentages also tell you something about how efficient the company is at generating profits.

Here again, beware of the gotchas. A company can artificially boost return on equity by buying back shares to reduce the shareholder equity denominator. Similarly, taking on more debt say, loans to increase inventory or finance property increases the amount in assets used to calculate return on assets.

3. Turn To Qualitative Research

If quantitative research reveals the black-and-white financials of a company's story, qualitative research provides the technicolor details that give you a truer picture of its operations and prospects.

Warren Buffett famously said: "Buy into a company because you want to own it, not because you want the stock to go up." That's because when you buy stocks, you purchase a personal stake in a business.

If quantitative research reveals the black-and-white financials of a company's story, qualitative research provides the technicolor details.

4. Put Your Research Into Context

As you can see, there are endless metrics and ratios investors can use to assess a company's general financial health and calculate the intrinsic value of its stock. But looking solely at a company's revenue or income from a single year or the management team's most recent decisions paints an incomplete picture. Before you buy any stock, you want to build a well-informed narrative about the company and what factors make it worthy of a long-term partnership. And to do that, context is key.

For long-term context, pull back the lens of your research to look at historical data. This will give you insight into the company's resilience during tough times, reactions to challenges, and the ability to improve its performance and deliver shareholder value over time.

Chapter 3 - Basic Information About The Stock Market

Taking your money and dropping it into different investment vehicles may seem easy. But if you want to be a successful investor, it can be tough. Statistics show that most retail investors those who aren't investment professionals lose money every year. There could be a variety of reasons why, but there is one that every investor with a career outside the investment market understands: They don't have time to research a large number of stocks, and they don't have a research team to help with that monumental task.

So the moral of the story is if you don't do enough research, you'll end up raking in losses. That's the bad news. The good news is you can cut down the losses as well as the amount of research you need to do by looking at some key factors investing. Learn more about the five essentials of investing below.

Research companies fully what they do, where they do it, and how. Look for the company's price-to-earnings ratio the current share price relative to its per-share earnings. A company's beta can tell you much risk is involved with a stock compared to the rest of the market. If you want to park your money, invest in stocks with a high dividend. Although reading them can be complicated, look for some of the most simple cues from charts like the stock's price movement.

Stock Market Basics Rule 1: Focus On Price

Educated traders follow a very different set of criteria. These traders focus on a single consideration: price. It may be a poorly run company but, if conditions call for a brief improvement in its price, it's a good buy for the trader who knows when to get in and when to jump out for a quick profit. Conversely, a great company will sometimes climb out of its comfort zone to a price where suddenly there are more willing sellers than buyers. This means the price is about to plummet, and it's the short seller who will reap the benefits.

Stock Market Basics Rule 2: Stay Liquid

There are two main components to this rule. First, the stock has to be actively traded at least 100,000 shares in daily volume. If trading stocks below that level, you run the risk of being stuck in a position simply because there are no traders on the other side. Second, you should stick to tickers with a price below $50 simply because the liquidity requirements above that level become distracting for most traders.

Stock Market Basics Rule 3: Practice Before You Jump In

This is arguably the most important stock market basics rule. Rather than investing in the broad market, you should consider following a few tickers and getting to know their trading range very well. Remember, this is a stock market basics approach that focuses on price. Once you know where it "should" trade then you'll be well-positioned to identify a departure from the norm and act quickly for a positive result. This is the opposite of "buy and hold" because you may load up on a stock in the morning, dump it in the afternoon or a day or two later, then buy it again when conditions change. It's an agnostic approach to the markets in which the most important consideration is your desire to be successful.

Stock Market Basics Rule 4: Don't Try to Out-Think The Markets

Here's a scenario you've probably witnessed: a company in a sector has a bad quarter, or maybe a product recall, and all stocks in that sector decline even though the other companies have done nothing wrong. It's illogical but that's how the market works. Similarly, mediocre companies will go up in price when the market is hot because "a rising tide lifts all boats".

When you're focused solely on price the basis of the patented trading strategy taught at Online Trading Academy you don't need the markets to be logical. You simply want to identify the zones where supply and demand are likely to be out of balance, then buy or sell when price enters these zones. Experience tells us there are large quantities of an unfilled buy or sell orders at these price levels and, once the orders are filled, the price will change direction regardless of what else is happening in the economy or the market.

The Basics Of Stock Types And Investment Strategy

Most people have two buckets of money in their lives. The first bucket is our income. It is what we live off, take vacations on, and run the household with. The other bucket is generally bigger and contains our wealth. To fill our big bucket we need a plan. We need to ask ourselves a series of questions and be quite specific about the answers.

- ❖ Why do I want to invest? What are my specific tangible goals?
- ❖ How old am I?
- ❖ How much capital do I have to work with?
- ❖ What are my strengths and weaknesses?
- ❖ How will I manage my risk?

Once we have the answers to these questions written down, then we can start to talk about the style of investing that we choose to fill our wealth bucket.

Types Of Stocks

There are two types of stocks: Common stock and Preferred stock. Briefly, common stock gives the stockholder voting rights, may or may not pay dividends and, if the company were to go bankrupt, would be paid after the bank and preferred stockholders. In contrast, preferred stockholders have no voting rights, own a fixed group of shares, earn higher dividends, and are paid before the common stockholders if the company were to go bankrupt. Learn more about Stock Types.

Investing Strategies

There are two traditional styles of investment: Growth investing and Value investing.

What Is Growth Investing?

Growth investing is taking advantage of new technological advances or medical breakthroughs with strong companies. Investing in stocks that have a lot of room for growth. This type of investment will often have high profit to earnings or P/E ratio. This is the style of investing Peter Lynch became famous for.

What Is Value Investing?

In value investing, you look for companies that have been beaten down, but still hold valuable assets that can be turned around into a profitable company later. Sir John Templeton, who was the master at Value investing, became a billionaire using this investing style.

What is Pro Active Investing?

ProActive Investing is a combination of growth and value investing, that also uses tools like options to reduce the cost of purchase, create revenue while you're waiting, and give you an escape route should the stock not move as you expected.

How To Invest In The Stock Market:

- ❖ Buy the right investment
- ❖ Avoid individual stocks if you're a beginner
- ❖ Create a diversified portfolio
- ❖ Be ready for a downturn
- ❖ Try a simulator before investing real money
- ❖ Stay committed to your long-term portfolio
- ❖ Start now
- ❖ Avoid short-term trading

1. Buy The Right Investment

Buying the right stock is so much easier said than done. Anyone can see a stock that's performed well in the past, but anticipating the performance of a stock in the future is much more difficult. If you want to succeed by investing in individual stocks, you have to be prepared to do a lot of work to analyze a company and manage the investment.

"When you start looking at statistics you've got to remember that the professionals are looking at every one of those companies with much more rigor than you can probably do as an individual, so it's a very difficult game for the individual to win over time," says Dan Keady, CFP, chief financial planning strategist at TIAA.

If you're analyzing a company, you'll want to look at a company's fundamentals – earnings per share (EPS) or a price-earnings ratio (P/E ratio), for example. But you'll have to do so much more: analyze the company's management team, evaluate its competitive advantages, study its financials, including its balance sheet and income statement. Even these items are just the start.

Keady says going out and buying stock in your favorite product or company isn't the right way to go about investing. Also, don't put too much faith in past performance because it's no guarantee of the future.

2. Avoid Individual Stocks If You're A Beginner

Everyone has heard someone talk about a big stock win or a great stock pick.

"What they forget about is that often they're not talking about those particular investments that they also own that did very, very poorly over time," Keady says. "So sometimes people have an unrealistic expectation about the kind of returns that they can make in the stock market. And sometimes they confuse luck with skill. You can get lucky sometimes picking an individual stock. It's hard to be lucky over time and avoid those big downturns also."

Remember, to make money consistently in individual stocks, you need to know something that the forward-looking market isn't already pricing into the stock price. Keep in mind that for every seller in the market, there's a buyer for those same shares who's equally sure they will profit.

"There are tons of smart people doing this for a living, and if you're a novice, the likelihood of you outperforming that is not very good," says Tony Madsen, CFP, founder of NewLeaf Financial Guidance in Redwood Falls, Minnesota.

An alternative to individual stocks is an index fund, which can be either a mutual fund or an exchange-traded fund (ETF). These funds hold dozens or even hundreds of stocks. And each share you purchase of a fund owns all the companies included in the index.

3. Create A Diversified Portfolio

One of the key advantages of an index fund is that you immediately have a range of stocks in the fund. For example, if you own a broadly diversified fund based on the S&P 500, you'll own stocks in hundreds of companies across many different industries. But you could also buy a narrowly diversified fund focused on one or two industries.

Diversification is important because it reduces the risk of any one stock in the portfolio hurting the overall performance very much, and that improves your overall returns. In contrast, if you're buying only one individual stock, you do have all your eggs in one basket.

The easiest way to create a broad portfolio is by buying an ETF or a mutual fund. The products have diversification built into them, and you don't have to do any analysis of the companies held in the index fund.

"It may not be the most exciting, but it's a great way to start," Keady says. "And again, it gets you out of thinking that you're gonna be so smart, that you're going to be able to pick the stocks that are going to go up, won't go down and know when to get in and out of them."

When it comes to diversification, that doesn't just mean many different stocks. It also means investments that are spread among different asset classes – since stock in similar sectors may move in a similar direction for the same reason.

4. Be Ready For A Downturn

The hardest issue for most investors is stomaching a loss in their investments. And because the stock market can fluctuate, you will have losses that occur from time to time. You'll have to steel yourself to handle these losses, or you'll be apt to buy high and sell low during a panic.

As long as you diversify your portfolio, any single stock that you own shouldn't have too much of an impact on your overall return. If it does, buying individual stocks might not be the right choice for you. Even index funds will fluctuate, so you can't get rid of all of your risks, try how you might.

"Anytime the market changes we have this propensity to try to pull back or to second guess our willingness to be in," says NewLeaf's Madsen.

That's why it's important to prepare yourself for downturns that could come out of nowhere, as one did in 2020. You need to ride out short-term volatility to get attractive long-term returns.

In investing, you need to know that it's possible to lose money since stocks don't have principal guarantees. If you're looking for a guaranteed return, perhaps a high-yield CD might be better. The concept of market volatility can be difficult for new and even experienced investors to understand, cautions Keady.

"One of the interesting things is people will see the market's volatile because the market's going down," Keady says. "Of course, when it's going up it's also volatile – at least from a statistical standpoint – it's moving all over the place. So people need to say that the volatility that they're seeing on the upside, they'll also see on the downside."

5. Try A Simulator Before Investing Real Money

One way to enter the world of investing without taking risks is to use a stock simulator. Using an online trading account with virtual dollars won't put your real money at risk. You'll also be able to determine how you would react if this were the money that you gained or lost.

"That can be helpful because it can help people overcome the belief that they're smarter than the market," Keady says. "That they can always pick the best stocks, always buy and sell in the market at the right time."

Asking yourself why you're investing can help determine if investing in stocks is for you. "If their thought is that they're going to somehow outperform the market, pick all the best stocks, maybe it's a good idea to try some type of simulator or watch some stocks and see if you could do it," Keady says. "Then if you're more serious about investing over time, then I think you're much better off – almost all of us, including myself – to have a diversified portfolio such as provided by mutual funds or exchange-traded funds."

6. Stay Committed To Your Long-Term Portfolio

Keady says investing should be a long-term activity. He also says you should divorce yourself from the daily news cycle. By skipping the daily financial news, you'll be able to develop patience, which you'll need if you want to stay in the investing game for the long term. It's also useful to look at your portfolio infrequently so that you don't become too unnerved or too elated. These are great tips for beginners who have yet to manage their emotions when investing.

One strategy for beginners is to set up a calendar and predetermine when you'll be evaluating your portfolio. Sticking to this guideline will prevent you from selling out of stock during some volatility – or not getting the full benefit of a well-performing investment, Keady says.

7. Start Now

Choosing the perfect opportunity to jump in and invest in the stock market typically doesn't work well. Nobody knows with 100 percent certainty the best time to get in. And investing is meant to be a long-term activity. There is no perfect time to start.

"One of the core points with investing is not just to think about it, but to get started," Keady says. "And start now. Because if you invest now, and often over time, that compounding is the thing that can drive your results. If you want to invest, it's very important to get started and have … an ongoing savings program, so that we can reach our goals over time."

8. Avoid Short-Term Trading

Understanding whether you're investing for the long-term future or the short term can also help determine your strategy – and whether you should be investing at all. Sometimes short-term investors can have unrealistic expectations about growing their money. And research shows that most short-term investors, such as day traders, lose money. You're competing against high-powered investors and well-programmed computers that may better understand the market.

New investors need to be aware that buying and selling stocks frequently can get expensive. It can create taxes and other fees, even if a broker's headline trading commission is zero. If you're investing for the short term, you risk not having your money when you need it.

"When I'm advising clients ... anything under a couple of years, even sometimes three years out, I'm hesitant to take too much market risk with those dollars," Madsen says.

Depending on your financial goals, a savings account, money market account, or a short-term CD may be better options for short-term money. Experts often advise investors that they should invest in the stock market only if they can keep the money invested for at least three to five years. Money that you need for a specific purpose in the next couple of years should probably be invested in low-risk investments, such as a high-yield savings account or a high-yield CD.

How To Choose A Stock: A Step-By-Step Guide

Step No. 1: Decide What Your Investing Goals Are

Different people invest for different reasons. Some are looking to build wealth for a life-changing event down the road, like retirement or a child's college fund. Others are looking for an income stream to provide spending money. Some want to speculate for a potential big gain, while others are just looking to preserve the money they already have.

Traditionally, the two opposite ends of the investing-style spectrum are growth and income. Chances are your investing strategy will fall somewhere on this spectrum. Growth investors tend to target, high-priced stocks, with strong growth rates and lots of potentials. Think Amazon.com or Facebook. Income investors, on the other hand, favor slower-growing, stable companies that pay dividends. Coca-Cola and McDonald's are good examples of top income stocks, often called blue chips.

Your investing goals will likely depend on your life situation. If you're a young adult looking to save money for retirement or a down payment on your first home, a growth strategy will probably be a better fit. If you're a retiree looking for money to supplement your income, choosing reliable dividend stocks would be better for you.

Step No. 2: Learn Some Stock Basics

Investing in the stock market can be intimidating for new investors. The stock market is full of confusing jargon, and the risk of losing money is very real. But it's not as complicated as it may seem. You only need to know a few terms to get a basic understanding of any stock. Here are three you should know:

P/E Ratio: The price-to-earnings ratio (P/E ratio) is the best indicator of how expensive a stock is. The actual price of a share, on the other hand, is relatively meaningless. The P/E is simply the price per share divided by earnings per share. It shows much investors are paying for a dollar of profits. Historically, the average P/E ratio is 15.7. Today, the S&P 500 P/E is 26.25. P/E ratios can range from none for companies without profits, to the triple digits for companies with slim profits and high prices, and single digits for companies in decline.

Revenue Growth: Revenue is simply the total sales of a company in a given period. Wall Street demands that essentially every stock show revenue growth or at least have a plan to do so shortly. While profits are more important to investors, profit growth can be more volatile and is often influenced by one-time events, making them more difficult to parse quarterly. Profit growth can also come from cost-cutting, which is not always in the best interest of the company's long-term growth. Revenue growth, on the other hand, is more straightforward and consistent, and generally gives a clearer reading of a company's growth prospects.

Dividend Yield: On financial news sites like Yahoo! Finance, annual dividend payouts are listed alongside percentages called dividend yields. The yield is the annual dividend payout divided by the stock price. It's the percentage of the stock's value that investors get paid back to them each year. The S&P 500's average dividend yield is 1.9%, while the best dividend-paying stocks pay 4% yields or higher. Note that most stocks pay out dividends quarterly, and many stocks don't pay dividends at all.

Step No. 3: Pick A Sector

Beginning investors will be best off picking stock in a sector they are familiar with. Love going to theme parks? Think about putting some coin into Disney. Have a medical background? Check out healthcare stocks. There are thousands of publicly traded stocks in the U.S. Narrowing them down based on your interests or experience can make a complicated process much easier.

Familiarity alone isn't enough of a reason to buy a stock, but it can give you an edge over the pros, and it will make it easier, even enjoyable, to follow the stock. You need to understand the underlying business, after all, to make smart investments. It's no surprise, for instance, that millennials recently flocked to Snap

Inc (NYSE: SNAP) shares after its IPO, as young people are by far the biggest users of Snapchat and therefore have the best understanding of the product. That doesn't necessarily mean Snap will be a winning stock, but those investors should have a better sense of the company's progress and when to bail if, for example, the product falls out of fashion.

Famed fund manager Peter Lynch encouraged individual investors to "buy what you know" -- a good first step for beginning investors.

Step No. 4: Bring It All Together

By now, you've decided what your investing goals are, learned the basic stock market fundamentals, and narrowed down your potential choices to a sector or group of stocks you're familiar with. Now it's time to pick one.

There are several factors to consider, such as potential growth and valuation (P/E ratio), but perhaps the most important question to ask yourself about a stock is whether it has a sustainable competitive advantage. Warren Buffett, the founder of Berkshire Hathaway and the world's most acclaimed investor, considers sustainable competitive advantage to be perhaps the most important criterion for choosing a stock. A sustainable competitive advantage will ensure that a company can continue growing and earning outsized profits, and stocks that have them will generally outperform over the long term.

Stock Picking: 7 Things You Must Know About A Company

While i'm not a huge fan of stock picking, I have made a few rather modest investments in individual companies. It's not something I do a lot of, but it is something I dabble in on occasion. If you decide that you want to try your hand at stock picking, it's important to do your homework. You want to choose something that's a good value especially if you plan to hold on to the stock for a while. As you consider your options, here are seven things you should know about a company before you decide to invest:

1. Earnings Growth

Check the net gain in income that a company has over time. Look for trends. Does the earnings growth generally increase? Even if the increase isn't dramatic, a company that has steady and consistent earnings growth over time can be a good bet for the future.

2. Stability

Every company is going to have periods where the stock loses value. This is natural, especially during times of economic difficulty and market upheaval. Instead, look for the overall stability as it relates to the economic conditions. Is there a great deal of fluctuation? If so, that could be a red flag. If, however, the company only seems to have real trouble when the rest of the market is struggling, you might do well to consider the stock.

3. Relative Strength In Industry

Take a look at the company's industry overall. Does the industry that the stock is in show promise for the future? If so, look closely at the company. What is the company's relative strength in the industry? Is it well placed against its competitors? Take into account the industry has a whole and the company's place in it.

4. Debt-To-Equity Ratio

All companies carry debt on the balance sheet. Even the richest companies carry liabilities. However, you want to be wary of companies with high amounts of debt. Look at the company's balance sheet, and compare the debt-to-equity ratio. You want a company that has more assets than liabilities. If you want an investment that is likely to present a lower risk, consider a company with a debt-to-equity ratio of 0.30 or below. You can look into companies with higher ratios if you have a little bit higher risk tolerance, or if a higher ratio is acceptable in the industry (construction companies, for example, are known for higher ratios since they use a lot of debt funding).

5. Price-To-Earnings Ratio

Consider how well the stock's price is doing concerning its earnings. The P/E ratio is often considered one of the most important considerations when it comes to fundamental analysis, and value investing. This ratio looks at the company's current price and compares it to the per-share earnings of the company. You figure the P/E ratio as follows: Take the current share price and divide it by the earnings per share. So, if a company is trading at $40 per share, and the earnings per share are $2.50, the P/E ratio is 16. Understand that the higher the P/E ratio, the greater the expectation that there will be higher growth in the future. While you don't want to rely entirely on this factor, it can help compare a company to others in the same industry.

6. Management

How well is the company managed? Do you feel that those in charge are competent? What is the general culture? Is the company is innovative? Also, consider whether or not a scandal could harm the company. Keep in mind, too, that some scandals only harm the company in the short-term. If the company is likely to recover from the setback, you can get a really good deal on the share price amid such difficulties.

7. Dividends

A company that pays dividends is often one with a certain amount of stability. However, be wary of companies with very high yields. That can be an indication of coming instability. Additionally, a company that pays a lot in dividends might not be reinvesting in the company. Look for companies that pay modest, but regular (and increasing) dividends over time.

8. Open Interest On Options Chains

Look at the open interest on options chains for a specific stock to see how many people are planning on buying and selling and at what price. This serves as an opinion poll on the stock's expected performance.

9. Insider Activity

Always consider the amount of shares CEOs and other executives are buying and selling, to get an accurate picture of what is happening on the inside.

10. News

It may be a good idea to avoid stocks that are constantly in the news. Stock prices will often reflect the investors' recent perception of the stock, which is usually not an accurate evaluation of the underlying, long-term value of the company. The dot-com bubble of the '90s is a perfect example

Factors To Consider When Buying Stocks

Finding the right price to pay for a stock or the best price to sell a stock is the way investors and new investors make money in the stock market. It seems obvious, but like many things in life, it is not easy to do. The first task is to buy at the right price, but what is the right price? Different investors will have different answers, but they would all agree that you should buy below what the future price will be.

Of course, figuring out what price the market will pay for a stock in the future is difficult. There are many ways to come up with a future price. However, since we can't know the future for sure, any future price is the best guess. You may have a better chance of coming up with a current fair value price, which is not the same as what the market is paying. Fair market value or intrinsic value is an assessment of what the business is worth as a going concern.

It considers the company's ability to generate free cash (cash remaining after all the bills are paid and current debt obligations satisfied). This is money the company can use to fund expansion, buy other companies, pay dividends, or simply bank for future use. Strong free cash flow is an important signal that the company has a competitive advantage over competitors. How big of an advantage (or economic moat) the company has played into deciding how strong the company's future looks.

Some Indicators To Consider

There are various things to consider when making investments in stocks. Here are a few that any investor should analyze when buying stocks.

Earnings

Look for companies that post year-to-year growth in earnings (an occasional hiccup during recessions is acceptable). While this is not a perfect metric (remember accounting charges can reduce earnings), it is one you should look at. Make sure the target company is reporting earnings substantially higher than its sector (you can find these numbers in Yahoo! Finance in the stock research section). Also, compare it to major competitors.

Free Cash Flow

Strong companies generate a lot of cash and, particularly, have a large flow of free cash. Free cash is what is left over after the company reinvests in itself to keep the business operating. Another way to think of this is how much cash you could pull out of the business without forcing a change in operations (closing plants, layoffs, and so on).

Return On Assets (ROA)

Return on Assets (ROA) tells investors the company is using assets wisely and creating value for the owners. How efficient is the company in generating earnings? Strong companies have a superior return on assets to their sector. For example, two companies each have $100 in assets. One company uses those assets to create $5 in earnings, while the other company uses the same amount of assets to create $15 in earnings. Which would you choose to own? Compare companies in the same sector for a valid check.

Return On Equity (ROE)

Another way to look at a company's profit-generating efficiency figures in how the company uses debt in addition to assets. Since most companies use some debt to run the business, it is important to consider it. Return on equity considers how well the company uses investors' capital and includes the debt. It is very important to compare companies in the same sector. If a company has an ROE that is much higher than its sector, be careful that something unusual is boosting the number (recent acquisitions, buying back stock, and so on).

Net Margins

A company's net margin is simply net income divided by sales. What this tells you is how efficient the company is in wringing profits out of sales. Some industries (grocery stores, for example) have low net margins and must drive a lot of revenue to generate profits. Other industrial sectors have higher net margins thanks to the nature of the business (software, for example). Great companies beat sector averages and close competitors.

Finding strong companies with strong futures takes some work, but investors willing to put in the time can be richly rewarded. Remember, strong companies with strong futures can be found in any industrial sector, so don't confine your search to the currently hot sector.

Profitable investing requires you to use a brokerage service that aligns with your investing goals, educational needs, and learning style. Especially for new investors, selecting the best online stock broker that fits your needs can mean the difference between an exciting new income stream and frustrating disappointment. While there's no sure-fire way to guarantee investment returns, there is a way to set yourself up for success by selecting the online brokerage that best suits your needs. In this guide, we'll break down everything you should look for in your ideal brokerage, from the obvious (like whether or not the platform allows you to trade the securities you're interested in) to the not-so-obvious (like how easy it is to get support from an actual human when you need it).

What Is A Stockbroker?

You can think of stockbrokers as conduits to the stock exchanges. In exchange for a commission on every trade, they send your orders on to stock exchanges and market makers, which do the heavy lifting of matching your buy order with someone who wants to sell, and vice versa.

You and I can't knock down the door to the stock exchanges and make a trade ourselves without a broker. In truth, the stock exchanges as we think of them from their depictions in movies and on TV don't exist today. Believe it or not, most trading takes place between computers located in dimly lit server rooms in New Jersey, a few miles away from New York City's financial district.

What Is A Stock Broker?

When it comes to investing in stocks, you can either buy and sell shares yourself (self-directed investing) or you can use an advisor and have your money managed for you (managed to invest). Way back when (the early 1900s), you had to use a licensed professional known as a stockbroker to place stock trades on your behalf. Thanks to the Internet, investors around the globe now invest for themselves using an online brokerage account. Today, "stockbroker" is just another name for an online brokerage account.

Types Of Stockbrokers

Just as the process for processing stock trades has changed, the terms we use for the people and businesses who facilitate trades have changed, too. Today, instead of using the term "stockbroker" as an all-encompassing term for any person or firm that deals in stocks, we generally divide companies into two categories: "discount brokers" or "full-service brokers," labels that better describe what they do.

Discount Brokers: Online brokers are discount brokers. They aren't in the business of giving you advice or phoning you up with stock picks. Instead, discount brokers simply focus on the very basic service of helping you buy or sell a stock (or another type of investment) when you want to from the convenience of your own home. Because discount brokers forgo many of the frills, they can price their services at rock-bottom prices. Many of the best online discount brokers charge $0 to place a stock trade, a bargain especially considering what traditional brokers charge. Also, discount brokers tend to have lower minimum investment requirements, some with no minimums at all, making them accessible for everyone.

Full-Service Brokers: Firms we label "full-service brokers" are more closely related to the stockbrokers of days gone by. Full-service brokers often employ human brokers who can help you make a trade, find mutual funds to invest in, or make a retirement plan. That said, full-service brokers are costly, since people are inevitably more expensive than computers. A popular full-service broker charges a minimum of $75 to place a stock trade, which can jump as high as $500 or more to buy a large amount of stock. Buying a mutual fund through a full-service broker can potentially set you back thousands of dollars since they often charge fees equal to a portion of the amount you invest. Full-service brokers are more likely to have higher account minimums; some advisors only work with clients who have $1 million in assets or more!

Realistically, the lines between the two types of brokers are slowly starting to converge. Discount brokers now have wealth management services that offer the help of a human advisor at a full-service price. Some full-service brokers also offer a basic level of service at discounted prices. Merrill Edge is the discount brokerage arm of the full-service brokerage Merrill Lynch, for example.

Ultimately, it comes down to how much service you need and what you're willing to pay. As self-directed investors who pick our stocks and funds, we're biased by own our experience -- we view the cost savings of a discount broker as being far more valuable than the personalized service of a full-service broker for our portfolios.

What Brokers Offer Fractional Shares Trading?

Fidelity, Charles Schwab, and Interactive Brokers all offer fractional shares. Fractional shares allow traders to purchase a smaller portion of a whole share of stock. For example, instead of needing over $2,000 to purchase one share of Amazon (AMZN), a trader could purchase a $100 fractional share (1/20th of a share). Fractional shares mirror whole shares, meaning if a whole share of Amazon increases in price by 5%, the $100 fractional share also increases by 5%. Fractional shares still receive dividends in proportion to the whole share owned.

What Are Fractional Shares?

A fractional share is a portion of a full share of a publicly-traded company. Traders can use fractional shares to gain exposure to high-priced stocks they otherwise might not be able to afford. For example, a trader with a $1,000 account balance could utilize fractional shares to own $400 worth of Amazon (AMZN), $300 worth of Apple (AAPL), and $300 worth of Alphabet (GOOG). Without access to fractional shares, Amazon (AMZN) and Alphabet (GOOG) would be too expensive to be included in this trader's portfolio.

What Is A Market Order?

A market order is an order to buy or sell a security at the current market price. Market orders are the most common type of order because they are easy to place. Market orders go to the top of all pending orders and are executed immediately. When markets are receiving lots of trading volume, the market price paid or received may be different from the quoted price when the order was initially placed. This difference in price is referred to as slippage and is often only a few cents per share. Investors tend to use market orders when they want to quickly purchase or sell a position. If an investor thinks a stock is going to go up multiple percentage points due to company news, he/she might place a market order to purchase shares of the company. In this instance, having the shares of the company outweighs the small price fluctuations that may come with placing a market order.

What Is A Limit Order?

A limit order is an order to buy or sell a security at a pre-specified price or better. A limit order helps lock in a set price in times of volatility. Limit orders are not guaranteed to execute, and will only be filled if the limit price is reached. Limit orders help traders avoid overpaying for a stock. They also help traders lock in a price when selling a stock. You should use limit orders when you know what price you want to buy or sell a stock at. Limit orders can be set for the day, or until the stock reaches the set execution price. Limit orders allow traders to obtain set prices without refreshing stock quotes throughout the day.

Top Features Of The Best Online Brokers

We recognize that one brokerage can't be the "best" choice for every single investor, so our view is that the best discount broker should thread the needle between offering the most functionality and perks at a price point that won't break the bank. The following features were considered particularly important in determining how to rank brokers you see in this list:

Commissions And Fees: The key advantage of any discount brokerage firm is cost. Investors now pay $0 commissions at most of the online discount brokers. In addition to a low price for every trade, we also prefer brokers who don't charge a monthly or annual fee just to have an account.

Account Minimums: We think having a low minimum account size is advantageous, particularly for beginning investors who plan to start small and add to their accounts over time.

Investment Choices : While most brokers offer roughly the same solutions for buying individual stocks on American exchanges, we think it's important for a broker to have a large selection of funds to choose from, too.

Research And Screeners: One key feature of having a brokerage account is that you can get access to a second opinion when you need it. Many brokers offer a full suite of third-party research as well as stock and fund screeners to help you sort through thousands of stocks and funds on key parameters like their price-to-earnings ratio, or the annual fees of investing in a fund, for example.

How To Pick The Best Broker For You

The best brokerage largely depends on how you invest. Investors who invest solely in individual stocks and ETFs would want to seek out different features than investors who use mutual funds alone, for example.

Researchers have concluded that an investor should own as many as 30 stocks to have a truly diversified portfolio. Thus, investors who want to build a portfolio of individual stocks may want to focus on the cost of trading, as the difference in price can add up quickly when investors place as many as 20 to 30 trades just to set up their portfolio.

Thankfully, most online brokers have eliminated trading commissions, but there are a few that still charge for stock trades, so be sure you know a broker's cost structure before you get started. Investors who use mutual funds or ETFs may want to prioritize a broker with a larger selection of funds to choose from. For example, E*TRADE offers thousands of mutual funds for investors to select from.

The best broker for mutual funds is a toss-up, as many regard Schwab and Fidelity as the leaders for the fact they offer more than 10,000 different funds. Schwab has thousands of no-transaction-fee funds with $100 minimums, which makes it a favorite for beginning investors without a ton of money to get started with.

Of course, convenience also plays an important role. Merrill Edge is a popular choice among investors who use Bank of America as their checking or savings account provider, since the two accounts can be easily linked, and the brokerage firm offers free trades to Bank of America customers who keep a certain minimum balance. With a full research department, Merrill Edge customers benefit from getting access to Bank of America Merrill Lynch research reports and more on more than 1,000 different companies.

How Much Money Do You Need To Start Investing?

While some brokers have minimum account requirements, the amount you need to get started as an investor has more to do with what you invest in than where you open an account. Here's how we think about the effective minimums for certain types of investments:

Mutual Funds: Due to the paperwork and backend work of maintaining accounts, many mutual funds have minimum investments of around $1,000, though there are some notable exceptions to the rule. Fidelity now offers some of its mutual funds with no account minimums, and even some funds with minimums will waive this requirement if the investor agrees to make automatic investments at regular intervals.

Exchange-Traded Funds (Etfs): One advantage of ETFs is that they trade like stocks, thus the minimum to invest in them is the price for one share. The largest ETF in the world, SPDR S&P 500 ETF Trust, which owns all 500 stocks in the S&P 500 index, trades for about $275 per share. Many other ETFs have lower share prices, trading for $100 or less.

Stocks: Just like ETFs, the minimum amount to get started investing in stocks is typically the price of one share. Shares of Ford recently traded for $11 each, while Facebook shares trade for about $200, and shares of Amazon traded for more than $1,700. However, Schwab recently started letting its customers trade fractional shares, making the higher-priced stocks accessible to investors with limited capital.

As we mentioned before, buying individual stocks at most of the online discount brokers will cost you $0 in commissions, which makes it very cost-effective to fill out your portfolio and less expensive to diversify with several stocks.

How To Choose A Stockbroker

Choosing a stockbroker can be more complicated than it sounds. The right broker can open up your investment opportunities, but the wrong one can limit your options and push up your costs.

There's a lot of information about different companies on this site and it can be hard to pull together when you're trying to pick one. So in this article, I'm going to look at 10 tips to bear in mind when choosing a stockbroker.

1. Decide Where You Want To Invest

If you only plan to invest in shares listed in your local stock market, then in most countries you'll have plenty of brokers to choose from. If you want to invest in some foreign markets, you may have very limited options. Check the international stock broker guide to see which firms will trade which markets. You can have accounts with more than one stockbroker and many investors do. But it's often convenient to try to get two or three comprehensive accounts covering most of your investments, rather than having to open a new account every time you want to buy a stock listed in a different country.

2. Check Costs Carefully

Many investors focus myopically on dealing commissions. But stockbrokers levy a wide range of costs and some will promise low headline dealing rates, only to claw it all back through high currency conversion costs or excessive account management fees. Read the guide to how stockbrokers charge and compare costs in the detailed stock broker comparison tables for the UK, the US, Hong Kong, or Singapore. Try to get a feel what it will cost you to run your portfolio over a year, rather than just the price per trade.

3. Decide What You Want From Your Stockbroker

Stockbrokers fall into three types. Execution-only or discount brokers simply carry out your trading instructions, either online or by phone. Most of the stockbrokers listed on this site are execution-only brokers. Advisory or full-service brokers will discuss your portfolio and investment ideas with you. You make the final decision, but they will offer you advice. And some advisory brokers also offer discretionary services for clients with large portfolios, where they will manage your money for you.

Advisory services cost more, but some investors appreciate the extra support and insight their broker can offer. Getting the best from an advisory stockbroker involves finding one that you have a good relationship with and can trust their advice. That isn't always easy. As part of this, you also need to think about how you plan to invest. Frequent traders will require high-speed online access and low commissions, while infrequent investors may be happy to deal by telephone and be less concerned about costs.

That said, while services aimed at long-term investors will never be suitable for traders, the opposite is not always true. There are plenty of companies that market themselves to frequent traders, but will still be a good and cheap service for those who trade infrequently. So don't be put off by the advertising.

4. Understand How Your Stock Broker Works

This point is a bit more technical, but it can help pick the best firm.

Different stockbrokers deal in different markets in different ways, especially when it comes to international stocks. A few offer direct market access, meaning that your order is sent directly to the exchange. More commonly, they trade through a market maker – a company that is always ready to both buy and sell a stock and constantly quotes a price to do either. Market makers only trade with institutions and stockbrokers, not directly with the public.

Depending on how your broker's firm is set up, this could involve it trading directly with the market maker. Or it could mean that they trade through another local stockbroker who trades with the market maker. The market maker they work with might be in the country you're trading or it might be elsewhere – for example, there are market makers based in London that will buy and sell American stocks with UK-based brokers without the trade ever going anywhere near New York.

As a regular investor, you probably don't care much about how it all works behind the scenes. And unless you need very fast trading and the absolute best price possible, it often doesn't make a huge difference to you. But obviously, the more intermediaries an order has to go through, the more the costs can mount up. So if you're going to be trading frequently in a particular market – as opposed to once in a while – you probably want a stockbroker who goes through fewer links rather than more.

5. Be Cynical About The Bells And Whistles

Some stockbrokers provide barebones services, offering trading services and nothing else. Others will send you regular research notes or have websites full of company fundamental data. Many include free streaming price data and some offer Level 2 data, usually at an extra fee. Some of this information can be very useful. However, much of it will be irrelevant to many investors – the long-term investor doesn't need to live Level 2 prices, for example. And you may well be able to get the same information either better or at lower cost through a separate provider. Think carefully about whether all the extras a stockbroker promises are worth much to you. You may be better off with you'd be better off with a simpler, cheaper firm and subscribing to the one or two things you need separately.

6. All-On-One Is Not Always The Answer

This is mostly focused on share dealing and in particular international share dealing. But many firms offer a wide range of other investment and trading services, such as a fund supermarket, contracts for difference (CFDs), foreign exchange trading, spread betting, and so on. It can be handy to have everything in one account – but be clear on what you're getting. In many cases, some of the services a broker promises are "white label" products – ie they are provided by a third party under the stock broker's name. That means you will often be paying two sets of fees – one to your stockbroker and one to the white label provider. If you want these services, you will often do a better deal by choosing your stock broker solely for its share dealing and getting your spread betting or forex trading account directly from the white label provider or another specialist.

7. Look For A Flexible, Convenient Service

At the same time, look for flexibility and range in the specific services that matter to you. If you're looking for a stockbroker, consider whether the broker offers tax-advantaged accounts, such as ISAs and SIPPs in the UK. Minimizing tax can make a big difference to your investment returns, especially for higher rate taxpayers. For international investing, a multi-currency account – which allows you to hold cash in several different currencies – is a must and should be provided without any extra charges. Most stockbrokers charge commission every time you convert from sterling to foreign currency and back again, so you want to minimize how often you do so. And see if they'll allow you to transfer in money that's already in the foreign currency you want to use. Transferring in money from a foreign currency bank account or using a foreign exchange specialist to do the conversion instead of letting your stock broker do it could save you quite a bit in commissions.

8. Make Sure You Like The Service

Regardless of how good a firm looks on paper, that counts for little if the online trading platform is slow and buggy, the telephones are always engaged or the customer service staff are unhelpful. I have dealt with several big-name firms whose guiding principles seem to be inflexibility, arrogance, and incompetence. Perhaps I was just unlucky, but I've heard similar stories from other users of the same companies.

With some of the leading stockbrokers, I'm amazed at how they manage to hang on to clients. Do not assume that being well-known and widely advertised means the company is any good. I recommend asking other investors for recommendations and searching online for opinions and reviews. However, remember that unsuccessful traders tend to blame everyone else for their mistake, so always assess how credible a review is.

Bad reviews are always likely to outnumber good ones because people are more motivated to review something that's gone badly. But if every review is awful and everyone is grumbling about the same problems, that may be a warning. There seems to be little connection between cost and service. Some of the ultra-low-cost providers offer outstanding service, while some relatively expensive ones are shambolic.

9. Don't Let Them Upsell You

Remember that a stock broker's business depends on how much commission and fees it generates. So they may try to encourage you to trade more often or sell your services and products you don't need. if you have a personal advisory broker or representative, their income is sometimes tied to the commission they generate. That doesn't mean that all of them will advise you to trade too much to benefit them – but bad ones will. Don't allow yourself to be pushed into something you don't want.

10. Stay Safe

Make sure you only do business with reputable firms and understand how investor protection rules and compensation schemes will and will not protect you if the worst happens. This article on opening foreign brokerage accounts, which I believe is a sensible step for some experienced investors. But you should always be careful and only make use of well-regulated firms. Never place your money with some dubious outfit that nobody has ever heard of based in a country that has no rules to protect investors. And this isn't just true when investing abroad – it applies at home as well. Only use companies that are fully regulated under your local securities law. And if someone cold-calls you try to sell you shares, put the phone down and report them to the regulator.

Best Online Brokers For Beginner Stock Traders

Here are the best online stock trading sites for beginners:

- ❖ TD Ameritrade - Best overall for beginners
- ❖ Fidelity - Great education and research
- ❖ Charles Schwab - Excellent research tools
- ❖ Robinhood - Easy to use but no tools

TD Ameritrade Best Overall For Beginners

Earning a recommendation based on its platform alone is E*TRADE. E*TRADE's web-based trading platform, Power E*TRADE, is an excellent environment for any beginner stock trader. It's easy to navigate, fast and includes usability upgrades perfect for new investors like paper (practice) trading and note-taking. There is no minimum deposit required to open an account at E*TRADE, and stock trades are free.

Fidelity Great Education And Research

Fidelity Investments offers new investors an easy-to-use website and excellent on-site education. Not only is Fidelity's learning center impressive, but Fidelity also does a fantastic job with its in-house market research and financial articles, Fidelity Viewpoints. Of all the brokers, I share and bookmark Fidelity Viewpoint articles the most. And, as far as subject matter goes, the broker's retirement education is exceptional. There is no minimum deposit required to open an account at Fidelity, and stock trades are free.

Charles Schwab Excellent Research Tools

Alongside an excellent selection of market research alongside an easy to use the website, Charles Schwab delivers a thorough educational experience that will satisfy beginners. Schwab's specialty is retirement, which makes it ideal for investors who want to take a long term approach to understand the stock market. There is no minimum deposit required to open an account at Schwab, and stock trades are free.

Robinhood Easy To Use But No Tools

For investors looking to conduct the bare-bones basics, Robinhood gets the job done well. Robinhood's mobile app is easy to use and ideal for newbies. That said, Robinhood provides little to no market research or trading tools to help beginners make better informed investing decisions. Drawbacks aside, Robinhood's no-frills approach to online trading is enough to earn it a recommendation. There is no minimum deposit required to open an account at Robinhood, and stock trades are free.

How To Buy And Sell Stocks On Your Own

To buy stocks, you need the assistance of a stockbroker since you cannot usually just call up a company and ask to buy their stock on your own. For inexperienced investors, there are two basic categories of brokers to choose from: a full-service broker or an online/discount broker.

Full-Service Brokers

Full-service brokers are what most people visualize when they think about investing well-dressed, friendly businesspeople sitting in an office chatting with clients. These are the traditional stockbrokers who will take the time to get to know you personally and financially. They will look at factors such as marital status, lifestyle, personality, risk tolerance, age (time horizon), income, assets, debts, and more.1 By getting to know as much about you as they can, these full-service brokers can then help you develop a long-term financial plan.

Not only can these brokers help you with your investment needs, but they can also assist with estate planning, tax advice, retirement planning, budgeting, and any other type of financial advice, hence the term "full-service." They can help you manage all of your financial needs now and long into the future and are for investors who want everything in one package. In terms of fees, full-service brokers are more expensive than discount brokers but the value in having a professional investment advisor by your side can be well worth the additional costs. Accounts can be set up with as little as $1,000. Most people, especially beginners, would fall into this category in terms of the type of broker they require.

Online/Discount Brokers

Online/discount brokers, on the other hand, do not provide any investment advice and are just order takers. They are much less expensive than full-service brokers since there is typically no office to visit and no certified investment advisors to help you. Cost is usually based on a per-transaction basis and you can typically open an account over the internet with little or no money. Once you have an account with an online broker, you can usually just log on to its website and into your account and be able to buy and sell stocks instantly.

Remember that since these types of brokers provide no investment advice, stock tips, or any type of investment help, you're on your own to manage your investments. The only assistance you will usually receive is technical support. Online (discount) brokers do offer investment-related links, research, and resources that can be useful. If you feel you are knowledgeable enough to take on the responsibilities of managing your investments or you don't know anything about investing but want to teach yourself, then this is the way to go.

The bottom line is that your choice of broker should be based on your individual needs. Full-service brokers are great for those who are willing to pay a premium for someone else to look after their finances. Online/discount brokers, on the other hand, are great for people with little start-up money and who would like to take on the risks and rewards of investing upon themselves, without any professional assistance.

Direct Stock Purchase Plan

Sometimes, companies (often blue-chip firms) will sponsor a special type of program called a DSPP, or Direct Stock Purchase Plan.2 DSPPs were originally conceived generations ago as a way for businesses to let smaller investors buy ownership directly from the company. Participating in a DSPP requires an investor to engage with a company directly rather than a broker, but every company's system for administering a DSPP is unique. Most usually offer their DSPP through transfer agents or another third-party administrator. To learn more about how to participate in a company's DSPP, an investor should contact the company's investor relations department.

The Basics Of Trading A Stock: Know Your Orders

With the growing importance of digital technology and the internet, many investors are opting to buy and sell stocks for themselves rather than pay advisors large commissions to execute trades. However, before you can start buying and selling stocks, you must know the different types of orders and when they are appropriate.

In this article, we'll cover the basic types of stock orders and how they complement your investing style.

Facts

- ❖ Several different types of orders can be used to trade stocks more effectively.
- ❖ A market order simply buys or sells shares at the prevailing market prices until the order is filled.
- ❖ A limit order specifies a certain price at which the order must be filled, although there is no guarantee that some or all of the order will trade if the limit is set too high or low.
- ❖ Stop orders, a type of limit order, are triggered when a stock moves above or below a certain level and are often used as a way to insure against larger losses or to lock in profits.
- ❖ It has never been easier for ordinary individuals to start investing and trading stocks.

- ❖ Several online brokers now allow you to open an account with low opening balances and low fees, some even with $0 commissions.
- ❖ Before you start trading on your own, you may also want to try out some strategies using a simulated or demo account first.

Market Order vs. Limit Order

The two major types of orders that every investor should know are the market order and the limit order.

Market Orders

A market order is the most basic type of trade. It is an order to buy or sell immediately at the current price. Typically, if you are going to buy a stock, then you will pay a price at or near the posted ask. If you are going to sell a stock, you will receive a price at or near the posted bid.

One important thing to remember is that the last traded price is not necessarily the price at which the market order will be executed. In fast-moving and volatile markets, the price at which you execute (or fill) the trade can deviate from the last-traded price. The price will remain the same only when the bid/ask price is exactly at the last-traded price.[1]

Market orders do not guarantee a price, but they do guarantee the order's immediate execution. Market orders are popular among individual investors who want to buy or sell a stock without delay. The advantage of using market orders is that you are guaranteed to get the trade filled; in fact, it will be executed ASAP. Although the investor doesn't know the exact price at which the stock will be bought or sold, market orders on stocks that trade over tens of thousands of shares per day will likely be executed close to the bid/ask prices.

Limit Orders

A limit order, sometimes referred to as a pending order, allows investors to buy and sell securities at a certain price in the future. This type of order is used to execute a trade if the price reaches the pre-defined level; the order will not be filled if the price does not reach this level. In effect, a limit order sets the maximum or minimum price at which you are willing to buy or sell.1

For example, if you wanted to buy a stock at $10, you could enter a limit order for this amount. This means that you would not pay a penny over $10 for that particular stock. However, it is still possible that you buy it for less than the $10 per share specified in the order.

There Are Four Types Of Limit Orders:

1. Buy Limit: An order to purchase a security at or below a specified price. Limit orders must be placed on the correct side of the market to ensure they will accomplish the task of improving the price. For a buy limit order, this means placing the order at or below the current market bid.

2. Sell Limit: An order to sell a security at or above a specified price. To ensure improved price, the order must be placed at or above the current market ask.

3. Buy Stop: An order to buy a security at a price above the current market bid. A stop order to buy becomes active only after a specified price level has been reached (known as the stop level). Buy stops are orders placed above the market and sell stop orders placed below the market (the opposite of buying and sell limit orders, respectively). Once a stop level has been reached, the order will be immediately converted into a market or limit order.

4. Sell Stop: an order to sell a security at a price below the current market ask. Like the buy stop, A stop order to sell becomes active only after a specified price level has been reached.

Market And Limit Order Costs

When deciding between a market or limit order, investors should be aware of the added costs. Typically, the commissions are cheaper for market orders than for limit orders. The difference in commission can be anywhere from a couple of dollars to more than $10. For example, a $10 commission on a market order can be boosted up to $15 when you place a limit restriction on it. When you place a limit order, make sure it's worthwhile.

Let's say your broker charges $7 for market order and $12 for a limit order. Stock XYZ is presently trading at $50 per share and you want to buy it at $49.90. By placing a market order to buy 10 shares, you pay $500 (10 shares x $50 per share) + $7 commission, which is a total of $507. By placing a limit order for 10 shares at $49.90 you pay $499 + $12 commissions, which is a total of $511.

Even though you save a little from buying the stock at a lower price (10 shares x $0.10 = $1), you will lose it in the added costs for the order ($5), a difference of $4. Furthermore, in the case of the limit order, it is possible that the stock doesn't fall to $49.90 or less. Thus, if it continues to rise, you may lose the opportunity to buy.

Additional Stock Order Types

Now that we've explained the two main orders, here's a list of some added restrictions and special instructions that many different brokerages allow on their orders:

1. Stop-Loss Order: Also referred to as a stopped market, on-stop buy, or on-stop sell, this is one of the most useful orders. This order is different because, unlike the limit and market orders, which are active as soon as they are entered, this order remains dormant until a certain price is passed, at which time it is activated as a market order. For instance, if a stop-loss sell order were placed on the XYZ shares at $45 per share, the order would be inactive until the price reached or dropped below $45. The order would then be transformed into a market order, and the shares would be sold at the best available price. You should consider using this type of order if you don't have time to watch the market continually but need protection from a large downside move. A good time to use a stop order is before you leave on vacation.

2. Stop-limit Order: These are similar to stop-loss orders, but as their name states, there is a limit on the price at which they will execute. There are two prices specified in a stop-limit order: the stop price, which will convert the order to a sell order, and the limit price. Instead of the order becoming a market order to sell, the sell order becomes a limit order that will only execute at the limit price or better. This can mitigate a potential problem with stop-loss orders, which can be triggered during a flash crash when prices plummet but subsequently recover.

3. All Or None (AON): This type of order is especially important for those who buy penny stocks. An all-or-none order ensures that you get either the entire quantity of stock you requested or none at all. This is typically problematic when a stock is very illiquid or a limit is placed on the order. For example, if you put in an order to buy 2,000 shares of XYZ but only 1,000 are being sold, an all-or-none restriction means your order will not be filled until there are at least 2,000 shares available at your preferred price. If you don't place an all-or-none restriction, your 2,000 share order would be partially filled for 1,000 shares.

4. Immediate Or Cancel (IOC): An IOC order mandates that whatever amount of an order that can be executed in the market (or at a limit) in a very short period, often just a few seconds or less, be filled and then the rest of the order canceled. If no shares are traded in that "immediate" interval, then the order is canceled completely.

5. Fill Or Kill (FOK): This type of order combines an AON order with an IOC specification; in other words, it mandates that the entire order size be traded and in a very short period, often a few seconds or less. If neither condition is met, the order is canceled.

6. Good 'Til Canceled (GTC): This is a time restriction that you can place on different orders. A good-til-canceled order will remain active until you decide to cancel it. Brokerages will typically limit the maximum time you can keep an order open (active) to 90 days.

Day: If you don't specify a time frame of expiry through the GTC instruction, then the order will typically be set as a day order. This means that after the end of the trading day, the order will expire. If it isn't transacted (filled) then you will have to re-enter it the following trading day.

Take Profit: A take profit order (sometimes called a profit target) is intended to close out the trade at a profit once it has reached a certain level. Execution of a Take Profit order closes the position. This type of order is always connected to an open position of a pending order

Successful Stock Market Trading Strategies

For many newly established investors, the prospect of actively trading in the markets can be intimidating. After all, it is almost impossible not to be overwhelmed by the sheer variety of investment platforms, assets, and lingo that are now an inherent element of modern investing. For many newly established investors, the prospect of actively trading in the markets can be intimidating. After all, it is almost impossible not to be overwhelmed by the sheer variety of investment platforms, assets, and lingo that are now an inherent element of modern investing.

Although mastering the markets may take years of patient study and practice, there are a variety of relatively straightforward stock trading strategies that you can begin using right away. These include growth investing, value investing, mutual fund investment, and IRA investments, among others. In each scenario, you should be able to make knowledgeable, well-researched trading decisions using market trading strategies that guarantee the best possible chances for a lucrative return.

Tip

Finding the perfect market trading strategies will largely depend on your current experience level and investing goals. Growth investing, value investing, mutual funds, and IRAs are all-powerful elements of modern trading strategies.

Growth Investing And Stock Trading

Generally speaking, growth investing is defined as the identification of companies that, through careful research, are considered to be capable of growing faster than the average index rate. The primary objective of growth investing is the greatest possible increase in the investor's capital gains.

In many scenarios, the companies identified in this strategy are evaluated based on a set of five parameters, those being:

- They have demonstrated a history of above-average earnings.
- Whether or not the company's forward earnings growth, or its anticipated earnings for next quarter, matches investor expectations.
- The effectiveness of management at controlling costs while simultaneously boosting revenue.
- The current style of oversight deployed by management.
- The likelihood that the asset will double in value within five years.

Evaluating a company based on these five parameters will allow you to gain a clear idea as to whether it would likely qualify as a viable element of a growth investment strategy.

Growth Investing And Emerging Companies

Another facet of modern growth investing is a selective investment in smaller, emerging companies whose current share price may not reflect the true potential of the company. For example, if an investor believes that a relatively small publicly-traded company has the potential to grow tremendously based on their products and services, they would likely qualify as a viable candidate for growth investing.

Keep in mind, however, that this particular element of the trading strategy can be somewhat risky due to a variety of reasons. Particularly in situations where a company has yet to deliver the product or service in question, it is entirely possible that the company could fail and the stock would be completely devalued, resulting in a total loss of investment funds.

It is also important to note that smaller companies will typically have a substantially lower trading volume than big-cap stocks. Because of this, it is quite likely that the stock will be subjected to increased volatility and may be harder to sell if prices start to decline rapidly.

Understanding Value Investing

Fundamentally, value investors seek to purchase stocks whose current sale price is below what the investors consider to be its inherent value. In many ways, value investing is no different than shopping sales. After reviewing available stocks, investors seek out selections that, for whatever reason, are currently undervalued.

A stock may become undervalued for a variety of reasons. For example, a general market downturn due to a loss of investor confidence could push the sale price of a stock below its intrinsic value. Other issues, such as disappointing quarterly earnings reports or media scandals, could also temporarily push the price of a stock below its current worth. It is in moments like these where value investors purchase the stock in question and hold the asset until its sale price returns to or exceeds its intrinsic value.

Important Data Points For Value Investing

Investors primarily rely on a stock's price-to-earnings ratio, also referred to as the P/E ratio, and its earnings yield. As expressed in the term itself, the P/E ratio is a quantitative measurement of the price a stock is currently selling for relative to the specific earnings per share reported annually by the company.

So, for example, if a stock has a P/E/ ratio of 10, this means that the current price of the stock is 10 times greater than the earnings per single share of stock the company has produced. As a general rule, value investors seek the lowest possible P/E ratio when selecting viable stock targets. This is because stocks with high P/E ratios may already be overvalued which would then likely lead to a price correction rather than growth. A stock is commonly considered a desirable investment opportunity for value investors if its P/E ratio is below 10.

Understanding Earnings Yield

Directly related to the P/E ratio of a stock is its earnings yield. Earnings yield is defined as the value of the earnings per share of a company for the most recent 12-month period expressed as a fractional amount of the current market price of the stock. Essentially, the earnings yield of a stock is the exact inverse of its earnings multiplier.

As an example, consider the following: A company has a 12-month earnings-per-share value of $3.75 per share. The current value of the stock is $17. To calculate the earnings yield, use the following equation:

(Earnings Per Share) 3.75 / (Current Market Price) 17 = 0.22.

For value investors, the higher the earnings yield, the more attractive the stock becomes a potential investment.

Beginning Mutual Fund Investing

For those investors who are hesitant about trading single stocks, a mutual fund may be one of the better market trading strategies available. By definition, a mutual fund is a collective pool of money that is actively overseen by a fund manager and is invested in various stocks, bonds, and other assets as part of a revenue generation strategy. An important early distinction to be made is that a mutual fund does not necessarily have to be composed exclusively of stocks. Many of the most successful mutual funds in existence today carry a highly diversified portfolio to hedge against various forms of market turbulence.

There are two basic forms of mutual funds open to investors today: closed-ended funds and open-ended funds. These two labels help define how investors purchase shares in the fund and how exactly these shares gain or lose value over time. Understanding this distinction will help ensure that you know exactly how your money is being invested.

Open-Ended vs. Closed-Ended Mutual Funds

If you are planning on purchasing a stake in a mutual fund, you may be surprised to learn that some of these shares are not available in the stock market. This is because open-ended funds have a virtually limitless number of shares available and are traded outside of the stock market. A fund manager running an open-ended fund can agree to take on as much capital from investors as they feel confident they can reasonably manage.

They accrue this capital through the issuance of shares, which are directly purchased from the fund itself. With this idea in mind, the prices of shares of an open-ended fund are not exposed to market activity in the same way that standard stocks are.

An open-ended fund's share price is fixed for a trading day, meaning that shares can be purchased throughout the day at the established price. Changes in share price will be a direct reflection of the net asset value, or NAV, of the fund itself. Once the price of the open-ended share is established, individual shares cannot be purchased for any other price during the trading session.

Pricing Closed-Ended Mutual Funds

The pricing methods used for closed-ended funds differ greatly from that of open-ended funds, due primarily to the fact that there are only a fixed number of closed-ended shares available. These shares exist in limited supply and are traded on stock exchanges just like any other stock. Shares are first offered to investors as part of an initial public offering, or IPO, just as they would be with any other stock. Once the shares have been created and offered via the IPO, no additional shares can be created.

Given the fact that these shares trade in the open marketplace, the price of a closed-ended fund share is influenced by investor sentiment just as much as it is by the actual value of the assets in the fund itself. Given the fact that closed-ended fund shares are traded in the public markets, the price of these shares can fluctuate significantly throughout a single trading day. Fluctuating levels of supply and demand typically result in shares of closed-ended funds trading above or below the net asset value of the fund itself.

Basics Of Investing In IRAs

Most market experts advise that newly established investors clearly define their investment goals before they begin trading in the markets. The reasons for this are relatively simple: if an investor knows what their desired result is before they begin trading, certain investment platforms may be far more conducive to reaching them.

As a great example, consider the topic of retirement. Many working adults invest in the market to help create a "nest egg" that they can use to sustain themselves during retirement. One of the most popular market platforms that are directly tailored to these goals is an individual retirement account or IRA. IRAs are unique in the fact that they offer specific tax advantages to investors in exchange for keeping their funds invested for an extended period.

Roth IRAs vs Traditional IRAs

Any discussion of IRAs will undoubtedly compare traditional IRAs and Roth IRA plans. In both scenarios, investors can deposit funds up to a federally mandated limit annually. Upon reaching the age of 59 1/2, account owners can begin withdrawing funds from their IRA. It is during this distribution process that the clear differences between Roth IRAs and traditional IRAs emerge.

With a traditional IRA, individuals can exempt the income they place in the IRA from their annual tax reporting. Essentially, these funds can be deposited directly into the IRA and are not reported as income on that year's tax return. However, during the distribution period, withdrawals from the account will be taxed at normal income tax rates.

This process is quite different from the Roth IRA, due in large part to the fact that individuals are required to pay tax on their Roth IRA contributions at the time the investment is made. In exchange, they are not required to pay tax during the withdrawal process. Given the fact that the funds in their account may grow tremendously throughout the account, an initial tax payment may be significantly less than the tax on withdrawal at a later point.

4 Common Active Trading Strategies

Active trading is the act of buying and selling securities based on short-term movements to profit from the price movements on a short-term stock chart. The mentality associated with an active trading strategy differs from the long-term, buy-and-hold strategy found among passive or indexed investors. Active traders believe that short-term movements and capturing the market trend are where the profits are made. There are various methods used to accomplish an active trading strategy, each with appropriate market environments and risks inherent in the strategy. Here are four of the most common active trading strategies and the built-in costs of each strategy.

Active trading is a strategy that involves 'beating the market' through identifying and timing profitable trades, often for short holding periods. Within active trading, several general strategies can be employed. Day trading, position trading, swing trading, and scalping are four popular active trading methodologies. Active traders can employ one or many of the aforementioned strategies. However, before deciding on engaging in these strategies, the risks, and costs associated with each one need to be explored and considered.

4 Common Active Trading Strategies

1. Day Trading

Day trading is perhaps the most well-known active trading style. It's often considered a pseudonym for active trading itself. Day trading, as its name implies, is the method of buying and selling securities within the same day. Positions are closed out within the same day they are taken, and no position is held overnight. Traditionally, day trading is done by professional traders, such as specialists or market makers. However, electronic trading has opened up this practice to novice traders.

"Active trading is a popular strategy for those trying to beat the market average".

2. Position Trading

Some consider position trading to be a buy-and-hold strategy and not active trading. However, position trading, when done by an advanced trader, can be a form of active trading. Position trading uses longer-term charts – anywhere from daily to monthly – in combination with other methods to determine the trend of the current market direction. This type of trade may last for several days to several weeks and sometimes longer, depending on the trend.

Trend traders look for successive higher highs or lower highs to determine the trend of a security. By jumping on and riding the "wave," trend traders aim to benefit from both the up and downside of market movements. Trend traders look to determine the direction of the market, but they do not try to forecast any price levels. Typically, trend traders jump on the trend after it has established itself, and when the trend breaks, they usually exit the position. This means that in periods of high market volatility, trend trading is more difficult and its positions are generally reduced.

3. Swing Trading

When a trend breaks, swing traders typically get in the game. At the end of a trend, there is usually some price volatility as the new trend tries to establish itself. Swing traders buy or sell as that price volatility sets in. Swing trades are usually held for more than a day but for a shorter time than trend trades. Swing traders often create a set of trading rules based on technical or fundamental analysis.

These trading rules or algorithms are designed to identify when to buy and sell a security. While a swing-trading algorithm does not have to be exact and predict the peak or valley of a price move, it does need a market that moves in one direction or another. A range-bound or sideways market is a risk for swing traders.

4. Scalping

Scalping is one of the quickest strategies employed by active traders. It includes exploiting various price gaps caused by bid-ask spreads and order flows. The strategy generally works by making the spread or buying at the bid price and selling at the asking price to receive the difference between the two price points. Scalpers attempt to hold their positions for a short period, thus decreasing the risk associated with the strategy.

Additionally, a scalper does not try to exploit large moves or move high volumes. Rather, they try to take advantage of small moves that occur frequently and move smaller volumes more often. Since the level of profits per trade is small, scalpers look for more liquid markets to increase the frequency of their trades. And unlike swing traders, scalpers like quiet markets that aren't prone to sudden price movements so they can potentially make the spread repeatedly on the same bid/ask prices.

Chapter 8 - Trading Psychology

What Is Trading Psychology?

Trading psychology refers to the emotions and mental state that help to dictate success or failure in trading securities. Trading psychology represents various aspects of an individual's character and behaviors that influence their trading actions. Trading psychology can be as important as other attributes such as knowledge, experience, and skill in determining trading success. Discipline and risk-taking are two of the most critical aspects of trading psychology since a trader's implementation of these aspects are critical to the success of his or her trading plan. While fear and greed are the two most commonly known emotions associated with trading psychology, other emotions that drive trading behavior are hope and regret.

The field of active trading is a challenging, fast-paced environment with nearly infinite possibilities and pitfalls. The odds are seemingly stacked against active traders in the marketplace, with studies suggesting that upwards of 80% consistently lose money and only 1% achieve predictable, long-term profitability. With four out of five traders showing regular losses, it's a wonder anyone is willing to pursue a career in the trading industry. After all, it's not typical for an individual to invest time and money into a business that has an 80% chance of failing. So, why the attraction to active trading as a profession?, The answer lies in the benefits that success in the marketplace can provide to prosperous traders. Financial independence, self-empowerment, and an escape from an unsatisfying career are a few perks enjoyed by those who beat the odds and grasp the brass ring.

What Is Trading Psychology?

Trading psychology refers to a trader's mindset during their time in the markets. It can determine the extent to which they succeed in securing a profit or it can provide an explanation as to why a trader incurred heavy losses. Innate human characteristics like biases and emotions play a pivotal role in trading psychology. The main focus of learning about trading psychology is to become aware of the various pitfalls which are associated with a negative psychological trait and to develop more positive characteristics. Traders well-versed in trading psychology will generally not act on bias or emotion. They, therefore, stand a better chance of yielding a profit during their time on the markets or, at the very least, of minimizing their losses. Trading psychology is different for every trader, as it is influenced by each individual's own emotions and pre-determined biases. Some of the emotions which impact trading are:

- ❖ Happiness
- ❖ Impatience

- ❖ Anger
- ❖ Fear
- ❖ Pride

How To Improve Your Trading Psychology

Improving your trading psychology can most easily be achieved by becoming aware of your own emotions, biases, and personality traits. Once you have acknowledged these, you can put a trading plan in place that takes these factors into account with the hope of mitigating any effect that they might have on your decision making.

As an example, if you are a naturally confident person, you may find that overconfidence and pride hamper your decision-making. For example, you might let losses run in the hope that the market will turnaround, rather than incurring a small loss on your trading account. This could lead to greater losses or the eventual collapse of your trading account.

To counter this, you might use stops as a way to minimize your losses and to make the decision about when to close a particular trade before you open the position. By doing this, you have become aware of your own biases and emotions as you have made a conscious decision not to act on them but rather, you have taken steps to combat them.

How Does Bias Affect Trading?

Biases affect trading as they are, by definition, a predetermined personal disposition in favor of one thing over another. As a result, they can hinder your decision making during your time on the markets because they might cloud your judgments and lead you to act on gut feeling rather than reasoned fundamental or technical analysis.

This is because trading bias means that you could be more likely to trade an asset that you have had past success on or to avoid an asset on which you have incurred a historic loss. Traders must be aware of their conscious biases as this can help them overcome them and approach the markets with a more rational and calculated mindset.

There Are Five Main Types Of Bias:

Representative bias means that you will stick to or be more inclined to replicate previously successful trades. You might do this without carrying out analysis for every trade of this type because, in the past, it has paid off for you. However, even if two trades seem similar, it is important to approach every trade on its own merits rather than on historical success

Negativity bias makes you more inclined to only look at the negative side of a trade, rather than acknowledging what went right. This could mean that you scrap an entire strategy when, in fact, you might only have needed to tweak it slightly to turn a profit

Status quo bias means that you will continue to use old strategies or trades rather than exploring new ones – you will stick to the status quo. The danger arises when you fail to assess whether those old methods are still viable in the current market

Confirmation bias is when you seek out or give greater weight to, news and analysis that confirms your pre-formulated ideas. It may also be that you don't seek out, or disregard, information which disproves your convictions

Gambler's fallacy is where you assume that because an asset has been increasing, it will continue to rise. There is no reason to believe that it should, similar to how there is no reason that a coin should land tails side up – rather than heads – after doing so a few times in a row

Emotions In Trading

Emotions are your worst enemy on the market and learning how to diminish their impact on your decision making is a rather tough task that can be achieved through years of experience. There are five common emotional mistakes that traders make and all of them have the potential to lead to massive losses, meaning you should do your best to overcome them. Those are the sensations of greed, fear, revenge, euphoria, and pride. So let's turn our attention to each one of them.

Greed

Greed is probably your worst enemy and is just as hard to overcome as fear itself. Greed is a typical human trait, one on which the whole human society is based, of course to some extent. Each person has an instinctive desire to do something better, even the laziest people, and to try to get a bit little more out of a certain situation. And although a small healthy amount of greed in life can be stimulating, there is no place for greed in trading, as even the desire to squeeze an extra 10 pips can be devastating, if an unexpected price reversal occurs on the way. Another common mistake associated with greed is that people tend to add too much to a position, simply because the market has moved in their desired direction, instead of basing their decision making on sound analytical reasons. And it is not just that, it is very common for inexperienced traders to risk too much right from the start, instead of scaling in and using a proper money management system. Another frequently observed mistake derived from greed is that newbie traders choose high leverage right from the beginning, drawn by the possibilities of high returns. Well, you can guess how that ends.

Euphoria

Euphoria is a variety of greed that arises after a trader has experienced a streak of winning trades or a single large winner. It builds an exceedingly positive sentiment and confidence, often luring you to enter and hold many new positions, usually in the same direction as the previous winner, which however can end badly. This is the reason why some traders experience their biggest losses right after they've had a good winning streak. It is very tempting to try and ride the winners wave immediately after you've earned some good profit, but you must keep your feet on the ground a draw a thick line between reality and the sensation that everything you do will turn to gold.

Fear

Fear is another overwhelming feeling, completely natural for each living creature, but unwelcome in a trader's mindset. Fear can cause you to miss on profits by exiting a winning position earlier, miss on opportunities by not entering a position at all, or induce losses when you exit a losing position too early and not give it a chance to turn profitable as your sound trading strategy had predicted. Like animals, people feel fear as they encounter a source of the threat, in our case the threat of losing money. Fear itself has a destructive power over your trading capital, but allowing it to get the best of you will then lead to further negative emotions such as anger, revenge, and hatred. Overcoming fear requires a lot of practice, discipline, and a lot of thinking beforehand.

Revenge

As mentioned above, revenge very often follows fear and the negative results it carries with it. For example, a trader might get agitated on missing a very good entry opportunity after having thought about it but decided not to enter due to fear of losing money.

"Revenge trading" commonly occurs after a trader experiences a loss, especially if it's greater than what he could usually handle. This once again calls out for using a proper money management system. Many market players commonly enter revenge mode after a trade, which they were sure will be successful, goes wrong causing the loss of money. There are two things to be considered here:

- ❖ There is nothing sure on the markets;
- ❖ Protective stops are your friend.

Pride

Pride is another major issue some traders encounter. It reflects a behavior where traders refuse to admit and recognize their mistakes, thus rendering them unable to learn from them and improve. The stubbornness of these traders drags them down and instead of getting better at what they are doing, they just worsen their performance. Not acknowledging your mistakes and being overconfident in your capabilities leads to poor risk management, without which, as we know, you are doomed to eventually fail. That is why (its a pattern), you must at all costs remain neutral and stick to your predefined trading strategy.

7 Tips To Avoid Emotional Trading

- ❖ Identify your personality traits
- ❖ Develop and follow a trading plan
- ❖ Have patience
- ❖ Be adaptive
- ❖ Take a break after a loss
- ❖ Accept your winnings
- ❖ Keep a trading log

Identify Your Personality Traits

One of the keys to developing successful trading psychology is identifying your personality traits early on. You will need to be honest with yourself and say if you have impulsive tendencies or if you are prone to acting out of anger or frustration. If this is the case, it is important to keep these traits in check while you are actively trading because they can lead you to make rash and ill-advised decisions that have little analytical backing. However, it is also important to play to your strengths. For instance, if you are naturally calm and calculated, you can take advantage of these personality traits during your time in the markets. Equally as important as identifying and being aware of your personality traits and emotions is recognizing your biases, as listed above. Biases are an innate aspect of human nature, but you should be aware of what your individual biases are before opening or closing any trades.

Develop And Follow A Trading Plan

Having a trading plan is paramount to ensuring that you achieve your goals. A trading plan acts as the blueprint to your trading, and it should highlight your time commitments, your available trading funds, your risk-reward ratio, and a trading strategy that you feel comfortable with.

For instance, a trading plan could say that you were going to commit one hour every morning and evening to trading and that you will never commit more than 2% of the total value of your portfolio to any one trade. This can help minimize losses and limit the effect of emotions on your trading as the rules for opening or closing a position are already highlighted for you. Trading plans should also take into account individual factors that could affect your trading disciplines such as your emotions, biases, and personality traits. If you make clear what your biases are before you start trading, you might be less inclined to act on them.

Have Patience

Patience is integral to discipline and you must have patience with your positions. Acting on emotions like fear can lead you to miss out on a profit by closing a position too early. Trust your analysis and remain patient and disciplined. Equally, when looking to enter a trade, it is important to be patient and wait for the opportune moment rather than just jumping into a trade right then and there. For instance, if you were wanting to speculate on some GBP currency pairs like EUR/GBP or GBP/USD, you may want to wait until just before a Bank of England (BoE) announcement as there tends to be increased volatility at this time.

Be Adaptive

While it is important to have a trading plan, remember that no two days on the markets are the same, and winning streaks don't exist in trading. With this in mind, you should become comfortable in assessing how the markets are different from day to day and adapt accordingly. If there is more volatility on one day compared to the day before and the markets are moving particularly unpredictably, you may decide to put your trading activity on hold until you're sure you understand what is happening. Being adaptive can help to limit your emotions and rule out representative and status quo biases, enabling you to assess each situation on its own merits – ensuring that you are pragmatic during your time on the markets.

Take A Break After A Loss

Sometimes after a loss, the best thing you can do is walk away from your trading account for a short while to gather your thoughts and compose yourself – rather than rushing into another trade in an attempt to regain some of your losses. The best traders are those that take their losses and use them as learning opportunities. They will typically take a few minutes to themselves before going back to their platform, using this time to assess what went wrong for that particular trade in the hope that they might avoid making the same mistake in the future. In doing so, they keep emotions like pride or fear in check by letting themselves cool off before approaching the next trade with a clear head and sound judgment.

Accept Your Winnings

Just as important as taking a break after a loss is to quit while you are ahead and take your winnings. A succession of wins or one particularly big win can make you feel invincible and you could subsequently rush into another position to try and do it all over again. You might even open a succession of new positions in the belief that none of them will fail because today is 'your day' on the markets. This could cause you to take unnecessary risks or diversify your portfolio too quickly without analyzing each of the respective markets. Happiness can be just as dangerous as anger during your time on the markets and, as such, it is important to recognize when it might be impairing your decision making or could be harming your trading psychology.

Keep A Trading Log

A trading log will enable you to record all of your losses and wins, as well as the emotions that you were experiencing during that particular trade. As a result, it is the culmination of all the previous points in this article and can be used to assess whether what you did at any one point in time was a good decision or not. For instance, a trading log can be used to record a time when you chose to cut your losses and the eventual price that the asset hit. By doing this, you can see if you made the right decision or not. Equally, it can be used to record when you accepted your winnings and if your emotions played a role in whether you chose to close that position too early or a little late.

Effective Trading Mindset Is Of Critical Importance

First, a trader needs to establish a plan for trading. This includes coming up with a plan on how to amass knowledge of the area (Forex trading), attending trading seminars, taking up online courses, and spending as much time as possible to research the matter. One should take his/her time to study variations of price charts, read interviews with managers, policymakers, experts, or day-to-day analysis in specialized media and why not even do macroeconomic, corporate or industry analysis of his/her own.

The more knowledge one obtains, the easier he/she could manage issues, such as fear.

Second, a trader needs to know his/her trading strategy to the last possible detail. He/she, just being acquainted with the strategy is not enough. Precision and complete awareness of what signals from the market to expect, to enter into a respective position, is obligatory.

Third, a trader needs to implement strict management of risk. If one does not follow the strict rule to manage risk on each trade, the chance to give in to his/her emotions eventually increases. The best way to protect yourself against the chance of becoming a highly-emotional trader is to risk only the amount, which you feel completely convenient to lose. This should be applied to each position one enters.

To expect a loss on any trade gives you the awareness that there is always a chance of such a scenario to develop, a chance of something unexpected to occur and adversely impact your position.

Fourth, an investor should abstain from over-trading. There is no need to trade way too much. One should simply know his/her trading edge (strategy) at one hundred percent and enter into trades, only in case he/she makes sure an opportunity is present.

Nobody's perfect. We are all going to have our wins and losses. However, some of the mistakes you might make when trading stocks are actually pretty common, and by no means reserved exclusively for you alone the majority of investors make many of the following mistakes. In fact, in some cases, the investor may continue to make the same mistake many times over, when they do not learn from their previous errors. Perhaps you have some direct experience with just exactly such a situation. The good news is that most of these mistakes can be avoided simply through awareness. We will take a look at the most common mistakes here, and identify ways in which may be able to stop the bleeding (or even turn them to your advantage).

Buying Shares In A Business Which You Do Not Understand

Too often investors gravitate towards the latest "hot" or fancy-sounding industry. They may know very little, or even nothing, about technology, or biotech, or the specific business the underlying company is engaged within. Of course, that does not stop them from trying to jump on to what they expect to be the next profitable train. In this scenario, the investor is overlooking all the advantages and benefits they would have over investors who know little about the industry itself.

When you understand a business, you have a naturally built-in advantage over most other investors. For example, if you run a restaurant you'll be in tune with businesses involved with restaurant franchising. You will also see first-hand (and before they become public knowledge) the habits of the patrons. By extension, you will know if the industry is booming, getting slower, or cooling down, well before the vast majority of investors.

To take our scenario a step further, by seeing the trends in the industry in which you are engaged, you should be able to spot some opportunities to make great investment decisions. First-hand knowledge, it would seem, can mean investment profits (or avoiding losses). When you invest in a company that is "above your pay grade," you may not understand the subtleties and the complexity of the business in question. This is not to say that you need to be a gold miner to invest in gold mining companies, or a medical doctor to invest in healthcare, but that certainly wouldn't hurt!

Anytime you can have an unfair advantage over most investors, you should press that advantage as far as you can. If you are a lawyer, you may do better with knowing when to invest in businesses that make their revenues through litigation. If you are a surgeon, you'll have a better understanding of how well (or poorly) a surgery robot is performing their task, and as such may have an inside track on how well the underlying stock may perform.

Expecting Too Much From The Stock

This is especially true when dealing with penny stocks. Most people treat low-priced stocks like lottery tickets and anticipate that they can turn their $500 or $2000 into a small fortune. Of course, this can sometimes be true, but it is not an appropriate mindset to have when you're getting into investing. You need to be realistic about what you are going to expect from the performance of the shares, even if such numbers are much more boring and mundane than the pie-in-the-sky levels for which you may hope.

Look at the performance of the stock up until this point. Also, watch all the other investments that are competitors in the same industry. Historically, has the underlying investment gained 5% or 10% per year, or have those moves been closer to hundreds of percentages? Do most companies in the industry see their shares moving 1% at a time, or is it more common for them to jump by tens of percentages?

Based on the previous performance, while not indicative of what may be to come, you could get an idea of the volatility and trading activity of the underlying shares. Typically, a stock will continue to act mainly as it has in the past, and usually, that will be inline with the overall industry.

Using Money You Cannot Afford To Risk

You would be blown away if you could see how different your trading style becomes when you are using money which you cannot afford to risk. Your emotions get heightened, your stress level goes through the roof, and you make buy and sell decisions that you otherwise would have never made.

An old Japanese proverb says that "you will eventually lose every dollar with which you gamble." You should never put yourself into the high-pressure situation where you are putting money on the line which you need for other reasons. The first thought is to only invest in speculative shares with 'risk money.' However, we can take it a step further, and suggest that you do not even use real money when you are getting started. Consider Paper Trading, which is no-risk, and requires no money whatsoever. Then, once you get good at Paper Trading, you can migrate towards trading real cash.

When you invest with money that you can afford to risk, you will make much more relaxed trading decisions. Generally, you will have much more success with your trades, which will not be driven by negative emotions or fear.

Being Driven By Impatience

We may have touched on the different emotions you can have when you're investing, but one of the most costly ones is impatience. Remember that stocks are shares in a particular business, businesses operate much more slowly than most of us would typically like to see or even than most of us would expect. When management comes up with a new strategy, it may take many months, if not several years, for that new approach to start playing out. Too often investors will buy shares of the stock, and then immediately expect the shares to act in their best interest.

This completely ignores the much more realistic timeline under which companies operate. In general, stocks will take much longer to make the moves that you are hoping for or anticipating. When people first get involved with shares of the company, they must not let impatience get the best of them... or their wallet!

Avoid These 8 Common Investing Mistakes

It has happened to most of us at some time or another: You're at a cocktail party enjoying your drink and hors d'oeuvres and "the blowhard" happens your way. You know he's going to brag about his latest "giant accomplishment." This time, he's taken a long position in Widgets Plus.com, the latest, greatest online marketer of household gadgets. You come to find he knows nothing about the company, is still completely enamored with it, and has invested 25% of his portfolio in it hoping he can double his money quickly.

Despite your resistance to hearing him drone on, you start to feel comfortable and smug in knowing that he has committed at least four common investing mistakes and that, hopefully, this time he'll learn his lesson. In addition to the four mistakes the resident blowhard has made, this article will address four other common mistakes.

1. Not Understanding The Investment

One of the world's most successful investors, Warren Buffett, cautions against investing in businesses you don't understand. This means that you should not be buying stock in companies if you don't understand the business models. The best way to avoid this is to build a diversified portfolio of exchange-traded funds (ETFs) or mutual funds. If you do invest in individual stocks, make sure you thoroughly understand each company those stocks represent before you invest.

2. Falling In Love With A Company

Too often, when we see a company we've invested in do well, it's easy to fall in love with it and forget that we bought the stock as an investment. Always remember, you bought this stock to make money. If any of the fundamentals that prompted you to buy into the company change, consider selling the stock.

3. Lack Of Patience

How many times has the power of slow-and-steady progress become imminently clear? Slow and steady usually comes out on top - be it at the gym, in school, or your career. Why, then, do we expect it to be different from investing? A slow, steady and disciplined approach will go a lot further over the long haul than going for the last-minute "Hail Mary" plays. Expecting our portfolios to do something other than what they're designed to do is a recipe for disaster. This means you need to keep your expectations realistic regarding the length, time, and growth that each stock will encounter.

4. Too Much Investment Turnover

Turnover, or jumping in and out of positions, is another return killer. Unless you're an institutional investor with the benefit of low commission rates, the transaction costs can eat you alive - not to mention the short-term tax rates and the opportunity cost of missing out on the long-term gains of good investments.

5. Attempting Market Timing

Market timing, turnover's evil cousin, also kills returns. Successfully timing the market is extremely difficult to do. Even institutional investors often fail to do it successfully. A well-known study, "Determinants Of Portfolio Performance" (Financial Analysts Journal, 1986), conducted by Gary P. Brinson, L. Randolph Hood, and Gilbert L. Beebower covered American pension-fund returns. This study showed that, on average, nearly 94% of the variation of returns over time was explained by the investment policy decision.1 In layperson's terms, this indicates that, normally, most of a portfolio's return can be explained by the asset allocation decisions you make, not by timing or even security selection.

6. Waiting To Get Even

Getting even is just another way to ensure you lose any profit you might have made. This means you are waiting to sell a loser until it gets back to its original cost basis. Behavioral finance calls this a "cognitive error." By failing to realize a loss, investors are losing in two ways. First, they avoid selling a loser, which may continue to slide until it's worthless. Second, there's the opportunity cost of what may be a better use for those investment dollars.

7. Failing To Diversify

While professional investors may be able to generate alpha (or excess return over a benchmark) by investing in a few concentrated positions, common investors should not try to do this. Stick to the principle of diversification. In building an ETF or mutual fund portfolio, remember to allocate an exposure to all major spaces. In building an individual stock portfolio, allocate to all major sectors. As a general rule of thumb, do not allocate more than 5% to 10% to any one investment.

8. Letting Your Emotions Rule

Perhaps the No.1 killer of investment return is your emotions. The axiom that fear and greed rule the market is true. Do not let fear or greed overtake you. Focus on the bigger picture. Stock market returns may deviate wildly over a shorter time frame, but over the long term, historical returns for large-cap stocks can average 10%. Realize that, over a long time horizon, your portfolio's returns should not deviate much from those averages. You may benefit from the irrational decisions of other investors.

How To Avoid These Mistakes

Below are some other ways you can avoid these common mistakes and keep your portfolio on track.

Develop A Plan Of Action

Proactively determine where you are in the investment life cycle, what your goals are, and how much you need to invest to get there. If you don't feel qualified to do this, seek a reputable financial planner. Remember why you are investing your money, and you will be inspired to save more and may find it easier to determine the right allocation for your portfolio. Temper your expectations to historical market returns. Do not expect your portfolio to make you rich overnight. A consistent, long-term investment strategy over time is what will build wealth.

Put Your Plan On Automatic

As your income grows, you may want to add more. Monitor your investments. At the end of every year, review your investments and their performance. Determine whether your equity-to-fixed-income ratio should stay the same or change based on where you are in life.

Have Some Fun Money

We all get tempted by the need to spend money at times. It's the nature of the human condition. So, instead of trying to fight it, go with it. Set aside your "fun investment money." You should limit this amount to no more than 5% of your investment portfolio. Do not use retirement money. Always seek investments from a reputable financial firm. Because some may compare this particular process to gambling, follow the same rules you would in that endeavor.

- ❖ Limit your losses to your principal (do not sell calls on stocks you don't own, for instance).
- ❖ Be prepared to lose 100% of your investment.
- ❖ Choose and stick to a pre-determined limit to determine when you will walk away.

Tricks And Tips

Investing in stocks does not need to be confusing or overwhelming. If you use some tried-and-true techniques, you can invest and monitor your investments without stress. Once you have learned a few tricks and tips for investing in stocks, you can put your money to work for you.

Determine Your Risk Tolerance

Before you put even one penny in the stock market, you need to know what kind of investor you are. For example, if you are near retirement and want to protect your money, you might have a very low tolerance for risk. You could look at blue-chip stocks, so-called because the companies that issue these stocks tend to be steady and reliable. The ones that succeed, however, tend to offer better-than-average stock returns. You might also be somewhere in the middle. For medium-risk stocks, you could consider established companies that have been growing but have only been on the market for a period of 10 to 15 years. Remember this simple formula for investing in stocks: risk equals reward. That means the higher the potential rewards, the higher the potential risks.

Diversify

Stocks come in categories or classes. For example, you can invest in medical stocks, manufacturing stocks, high-tech stocks, and steel stocks, to give a few examples. Each type of industry has its ups and downs, and the companies in those industries seldom buck the trend. For example, if the manufacturing sector as a whole experience a decline, manufacturing stocks most likely will, too. Begin your investing program by choosing a variety of industries to invest in, so that if one goes down, the rest of your portfolio has a chance to make up for it.

Homework

Don't buy blindly. Many financial websites offer information on companies and their stocks. You can also find plenty of information on a company's website. Look at the stock's history, learn about the company's financial performance and management team, and research what professional stock analysts have to say about the stock and its potential for a higher value.

Avoid Overtrading

Once you make investment decisions, don't nervously debate whether or not you should sell the stock. Certainly, you might learn something that makes you think the stock is not as good an investment as you thought it would be, and you have every right to sell such stock. However, don't let your hopes rise and fall with every peak and valley in the stock's chart. Expect ups and downs, but look for a general upward trend to develop.

Learn Fundamentals vs. Technical Aspects

People who use stock charts are called "technical traders." Technical traders make investment decisions based on how the stock charts look. For example, if a stock chart shows a bigger-than-average decline in price on higher-than-average volume, many technical traders would sell this stock because they figure it will go down further. After all, so many sellers are getting rid of it quickly. People who study company profitability and sales are called "fundamental traders." A fundamental trader examines the company that issues the stock, looking for low debt, steady profits, sales growth, and expansion plans. Starting, use both approaches until you decide what fits best with your personality. Many investors have had success with both approaches.

Get Free Stock Charts

Many online services, such as StockCharts.com, offer free stock charts. Some of the major search engines also provide free stock charts as well as tutorials that teach you how to read charts and make your calculations. You can get advanced options for your charts and begin learning how a successful stock looks when it is charted.

Treat It Like A Job

Your money is important. Set aside sometime each day to study the markets, learn more about investing, and monitor how your stocks are doing.

Add To Your Portfolio

Keep adding to your portfolio regularly, so that you have more money to invest. Your portfolio will grow along with your investment knowledge. One way to do this is to set aside savings each month and wait until you have at least $1,000 to invest. Next, buy a new stock or add to your holdings in a stock you already own. Most brokers charge trading fees on a per-trade basis, so buying at least $1,000 worth of stock can keep the percentage of your trading fees down. For example, if you buy $500 worth of stock and pay a $10 trading fee, then a few weeks later by another $500 worth of the same stock and pay a $10 trading fee, you paid $20 to buy $1,000 worth of stock. That's 2 percent. Instead, make one trade for $1,000 and pay only $10, or 1 percent of your total trade.

Buy Late

You don't have to be in at the beginning of an uptrend. Let everyone else take a chance, and then when you determine that a stock's rise has staying power, you can buy. This can help you avoid fake rallies where a stock looks great and then tumbles quickly. A stock that rises in price 2 or 3 percent, levels out, then rises another 2 or 3 percent before resting again, may have staying power. A stock that shoots up suddenly over two or their days then drops dramatically, maybe confusing investors and could lack the power to climb steadily.

6 Stock Market Investing Tips & Guide For Beginners

Tips For Stock Market Investing

Everyone is looking for a quick and easy way to riches and happiness. It seems to be human nature to constantly search for a hidden key or some esoteric bit of knowledge that suddenly leads to the end of the rainbow or a winning lottery ticket.

While some people do buy winning tickets or a common stock that quadruples or more in a year, it is extremely unlikely, since relying upon luck is an investment strategy that only the foolish or most desperate would choose to follow. In our quest for success, we often overlook the most powerful tools available to us: time and the magic of compounding interest. Investing regularly, avoiding unnecessary financial risk, and letting your money work for you over the years and decades is a certain way to amass significant assets.

Here Are Several Tips That Should Be Followed By Beginning Investors.

1. Set Long-Term Goals

Why are you considering investing in the stock market? Will you need your cash back in six months, a year, five years, or longer? Are you saving for retirement, for future college expenses, to purchase a home, or to build an estate to leave to your beneficiaries?

Before investing, you should know your purpose and the likely time in the future you may need the funds. If you are likely to need your investment returned within a few years, consider another investment; the stock market with its volatility provides no certainty that all of your capital will be available when you need it.

By knowing how much capital you will need and the future point in time when you will need it, you can calculate how much you should invest and what kind of return on your investment will be needed to produce the desired result. To estimate how much capital you are likely to need for retirement or future college expenses, use one of the free financial calculators available over the Internet.

Retirement calculators, ranging from the simple to the more complex including integration with future Social Security benefits, are available at Kiplinger, Bankrate, and MSN Money. Similar college cost calculators are available at CNNMoney and TimeValue. Many stock brokerage firms offer similar calculators. Remember that the growth of your portfolio depends upon three interdependent factors:

- ❖ The capital you invest
- ❖ The amount of net annual earnings on your capital
- ❖ The number of years or period of your investment
- ❖ Ideally, you should start saving as soon as possible, save as much as you can, and receive the highest return possible consistent with your risk philosophy.

Pro Tip: If you're looking for a tool to help you research potential investments, sign up for Atom Finance. It's free, and it gives you access to real-time price quotes, professional-grade news, and analysis on companies, and it integrates seamlessly with your brokerage account. Sign up for Atom Finance.

2. Understand Your Risk Tolerance

Risk tolerance is a psychological trait that is genetically based but positively influenced by education, income, and wealth (as these increase, risk tolerance appears to increase slightly) and negatively by age (as one gets older, risk tolerance decreases). Your risk tolerance is how you feel about risk and the degree of anxiety you feel when risk is present. In psychological terms, risk tolerance is defined as "the extent to which a person chooses to risk experiencing a less favorable outcome in the pursuit of a more favorable outcome." In other words, would you risk $100 to win $1,000? Or $1,000 to win $1,000? All humans vary in their risk tolerance, and there is no "right" balance.

Risk tolerance is also affected by one's perception of risk. For example, flying in an airplane or riding in a car would have been perceived as very risky in the early 1900s, but less so today as flight and automobile travel are common occurrences. Conversely, most people today would feel that riding a horse might be dangerous with a good chance of falling or being bucked off because few people are around horses.

The idea of perception is important, especially in investing. As you gain more knowledge about investments – for example, how stocks are bought and sold, how much volatility (price change) is usually present, and the difficulty or ease of liquidating an investment – you are likely to consider stock investments to have less risk than you thought before making your first purchase. As a consequence, your anxiety when investing is less intense, even though your risk tolerance remains unchanged because your perception of the risk has evolved.

By understanding your risk tolerance, you can avoid those investments which are likely to make you anxious. Generally speaking, you should never own an asset which keeps you from sleeping at night. Anxiety stimulates fear which triggers emotional responses (rather than logical responses) to the stressor. During periods of financial uncertainty, the investor who can retain a cool head and follows an analytical decision process invariably comes out ahead.

3. Diversify Your Investments

Experienced investors such as Buffett eschew stock diversification in the confidence that they have performed all of the necessary research to identify and quantify their risk. They are also comfortable that they can identify any potential perils that will endanger their position, and will be able to liquidate their investments before taking a catastrophic loss. Andrew Carnegie is reputed to have said, "The safest investment strategy is to put all of your eggs in one basket and watch the basket." That said, do not make the mistake of thinking you are either Buffett or Carnegie – especially in your first years of investing.

The popular way to manage risk is to diversify your exposure. Prudent investors own stocks of different companies in different industries, sometimes in different countries, with the expectation that a single bad event will not affect all of their holdings or will otherwise affect them to different degrees.

Imagine owning stocks in five different companies, each of which you expect to continually grow profits. Unfortunately, circumstances change. At the end of the year, you might have two companies (A & B) that have performed well so their stocks are up 25% each. The stock of two other companies (C & D) in a different industry is up 10% each, while the fifth company's (E) assets were liquidated to pay off a massive lawsuit.

Diversification allows you to recover from the loss of your total investment (20% of your portfolio) by gains of 10% in the two best companies (25% x 40%) and 4% in the remaining two companies (10% x 40%). Even though your overall portfolio value dropped by 6% (20% loss minus 14% gain), it is considerably better than having been invested solely in company E.

Pro Tip: Another way to make sure your portfolio is diversified is to invest in different types of investments. Some people like to mix things up by investing in fine art through Masterworks. Blue-chip art returned 10.6% in 2018 compared to a 5.1% loss for the S&P 500. Others choose to invest in real estate through a company like DiversyFund.

4. Control Your Emotions

The biggest obstacle to stock market profits is an inability to control one's emotions and make logical decisions. In the short-term, the prices of companies reflect the combined emotions of the entire investment community. When a majority of investors are worried about a company, its stock price is likely to decline; when a majority feel positive about the company's future, its stock price tends to rise.

A person who feels negative about the market is called a "bear," while their positive counterpart is called a "bull." During market hours, the constant battle between the bulls and the bears is reflected in the constantly changing price of securities. These short-term movements are driven by rumors, speculations, and hopes – emotions – rather than logic and systematic analysis of the company's assets, management, and prospects.

Stock prices moving contrary to our expectations create tension and insecurity. Should I sell my position and avoid a loss? Should I keep the stock, hoping that the price will rebound? Should I buy more?

Even when the stock price has performed as expected, there are questions: Should I take a profit now before the price falls? Should I keep my position since the price is likely to go higher? Thoughts like these will flood your mind, especially if you constantly watch the price of a security, eventually building to a point that you will take action. Since emotions are the primary driver of your action, it will probably be wrong.

When you buy a stock, you should have a good reason for doing so and an expectation of what the price will do if the reason is valid. At the same time, you should establish the point at which you will liquidate your holdings, especially if your reason is proven invalid or if the stock doesn't react as expected when your expectation has been met. In other words, have an exit strategy before you buy the security and execute that strategy unemotionally.

5. Handle Basics First

Before making your first investment, take the time to learn the basics about the stock market and the individual securities composing the market. There is an adage: It is not a stock market, but a market of stocks. Unless you are purchasing an exchange-traded fund (ETF), your focus will be upon individual securities, rather than the market as a whole. There are few times when every stock moves in the same direction; even when the averages fall by 100 points or more, the securities of some companies will go higher in price.

The areas with which you should be familiar before making your first purchase include:

Financial Metrics And Definitions: Understand the definitions of metrics such as the P/E ratio, earnings per share (EPS), return on equity (ROE), and compound annual growth rate (CAGR). Knowing how they are calculated and having the ability to compare different companies using these metrics and others is critical.

Popular Methods Of Stock Selection And Timing: You should understand how "fundamental" and "technical" analyses are performed, how they differ, and where each is best suited in a stock market strategy.

Stock Market Order Types: Know the difference between market orders, limit order, stop market orders, stop-limit orders, trailing stop-loss orders, and other types commonly used by investors.

Different Types Of Investment Accounts: While cash accounts are the most common, margin accounts are required by regulations for certain kinds of trades. You should understand how margin is calculated and the difference between initial and maintenance margin requirements.

Knowledge And Risk Tolerance Are Linked: As Warren Buffett said, "Risk comes from not knowing what you are doing."

6. Avoid Leverage

Leverage simply means the use of borrowed money to execute your stock market strategy. In a margin account, banks and brokerage firms can loan you money to buy stocks, usually 50% of the purchase value. In other words, if you wanted to buy 100 shares of a stock trading at $100 for a total cost of $10,000, your brokerage firm could loan you $5,000 to complete the purchase.

The use of borrowed money "levers" or exaggerates the result of price movement. Suppose the stock moves to $200 a share and you sell it. If you had used your own money exclusively, your return would be 100% on your investment [($20,000 - $10,000)/$10,000]. If you had borrowed $5,000 to buy the stock and sold at $200 per share, your return would be 300 % [(20,000-$5,000)/$5,000] after repaying the $5,000 loan and excluding the cost of interest paid to the broker.

It sounds great when the stock moves up but consider the other side. Suppose the stock fell to $50 per share rather than doubling to $200, your loss would be 100% of your initial investment, plus the cost of interest to the broker [($5,000-$5,000)/$5,000].

Leverage is a tool, neither good nor bad. However, it is a tool best used after you gain experience and confidence in your decision-making abilities. Limit your risk when you are starting to ensure you can profit over the long term.

Conclusion

You can make a lot of money investing in stocks or trading in the stock market, but it is not something for the new investors. Care must be taken when it comes to stock investments. The investor must have a solid understanding of stocks and how they trade in the market or risk losing money in a volatile type of investment.

Let's Review What We've Learned In This Article :

- ❖ Having stock in a company means you are an owner. How many shares of stock you have determines the extent of that ownership. As part owner, you receive dividends and have voting rights.
- ❖ A stock represents equity, while bonds are debt. Bonds are low-risk investment vehicles with guaranteed returns, while stocks involve more risk. This is why stocks have a higher rate of return compared to bonds.
- ❖ In investing, the riskier the investment the bigger the chance of making more money. Investing in stocks can make you lots of money if you invest in the right company. However, you can lose all of it too.
- ❖ The purchase of stocks is commonly done through a brokerage. You can also get a dividend reinvestment plan (DRIP).

- ❖ Stocks are volatile. Prices change according to supply and demand. Many people have different opinions on why stock prices move the way they do. One of the most important factors that influence prices is earnings.
- ❖ Learning how to read stock tables or a stock quote is a must if you are planning to be a serious investor in stocks.
- ❖ It is not hard to read a stock quote once you know what the different terms and symbols stand for.
- ❖ Always remember the old stock market saying: "Bulls make money, bears make money, but pigs get slaughtered!". This will perhaps save you many times from losing your investment.

Investing in the stock market can be very rewarding, especially if you avoid some of the pitfalls that most new investors experience when starting. Beginners should find an investing plan that works for them and stick to it through good times and bad.

Even if you're not a numbers person, you shouldn't just ignore financial ratios when investing. Instead of staring blindly at them, look for a story. Every single part of a company's financial statement and every ratio gives you insight into the real-life performance of a business. Use an online brokerage firm if you need help. If you can invest in good businesses, you should make money in the long term. You shouldn't invest based on the result of one ratio alone. But when you add ratios to the total package of

Printed by Libri Plureos GmbH in Hamburg, Germany

quantitative, fundamental, and technical analyses, they could be a major source of success for your investments.

Ideally, you will not be committing too many of these common errors. However, the fact of the matter is that the majority of investors, in most cases, will continually fall back to making some of the mistakes which we've discussed in the article above. Luckily, you can use your losses and mistakes to learn how to avoid them next time. Most people learn more from their losses than they do from their gains. Given enough time, and a sufficient number of bad trades, you will be in a much superior (and more profitable) situation. Ideally, you will phase out the common mistakes quickly enough that you still have a big part of your portfolio left on the other side. Then, with your newfound 'enhanced' wisdom, you should be able to start gathering some profits!

9 781801 886123